The Forgotten History Of The American Jews In The United States 1770 - 1865

by David Pollock

Published by Pollock Publications (732) 741-5788 Fax (732) 741-5459
E-mail: dpoll55555@aol.com.

ISBN 0-9660512-0-3

LCC Card Number 92540

10 9 8 7 6 5 4 3 2 1

*This book is dedicated to
a wonderful and independent lady,
my wife, Ann Pollock.*

Contents

LIST OF ILLUSTRATIONS

Page

Preface _____

Historians often omit the history of minorities, particularly Jews and other minorities. This book is an attempt to show what the Jews accomplished and contributed during the period 1770 to 1865.

In this book we will see the friendship and amiable relations of President George Washington and President Abraham Lincoln towards the Jewish people.

It is an informative study of the Jews on both sides of the Revolution, on both sides of the slavery issue. This history has been neglected and not readily available in local public libraries. Jewish history books in many cases are out of print. One can search through almost all the myriads of textbooks of Lincoln and the Civil War and find not one mention of the friendship of President Lincoln toward his chiropodist, A. Zacharie and Abraham Jonas, the lawyer, both Jews.

Also the contributions of the small number of Jews in the American Revolution is completely unheard of in the general population. You will see in the emerging nation, Jews would have the freedom to participate in public life and at the same time build their communal and religious life as Jews. This was completely unheard of before this time.

This book, therefore, provides a short analysis of this Jewish American history in the hope not only of teaching some of the basics of Jewish American history but also will encourage readers to dig deeply into this history, perhaps from the bibliography and other sources that may be available.

I appreciate the help and generosity of the Jewish Archives in Cincinnati, Ohio and the American Jewish Historical Society of Waltham, Massachusetts. Also to Mrs. Mildred Howitt, librarian of the Congregation B'nai Israel Synagogue, professors Carl Calendar and Jack Needle of Brookdale College.

For the purpose of this book a Jew is a person who believes he is a Jew.

"Remember the days of old" from the Pentateuch.

Plaque commemorating Francis Salvador.
Courtesy, South Carolina Historical Society, Charleston.

Chapter I _____

Forgotten Jews of the American Revolution

The government of the United States which gives to bigotry no sanction, to persecution no assistance.   G. Washington

How many of us have heard about the Jews in the American Revolution? We heard much about Haym Salomon as being the chief financial support of the Revolution. Most historians believe his financial support for the Revolution was exaggerated though he was a great patriot.

In 1776, there were five Jewish communities with congregations in the United States. They were Newport, R.I., New York City, Philadelphia, Pa., Charleston, S.C., and Savannah, Ga.

Jews did make a mark in the Revolution out of all proportion to their population, which was about 3000 out of two and a half million in the entire thirteen colonies. Jews, I believe, are the unrecognized patriots of the Revolution, a past of which we have been largely deprived. I hope I can dispel that in this chapter.

In this chapter, the part of the rebellious Jews, and the Loyalists, who opposed the Revolution, will be discussed. Also, the effect that Haym Salomon and George Washington had on the Jews of that era will be shown.

Jews, about 200, actually fought in the Revolution and were mainly privates, non-commissioned officers, and even colonels. This was remarkable as the Jews had no tradition of military service at that time, and mostly were young.

On one occasion, a Jew, Mordecai Sheftal, a name that was prominent in Jewish history through the 19th century, helped organize the Revolution in Georgia by rallying the patriots and discrediting the Loyalists. He organized a group to secretly board a British ship in the harbor and remove the gunpowder, 15,000 weight, and much of the king's stores on board and then send it to George Washington's army in Boston. Other Jews in Georgia helped open the British blockade of the Savannah harbor to allow the French troops to enter. Sheftal remained loyal throughout the Revolution. He was named to the general staff of the Georgia Brigade with the rank of colonel. Even his son, only seventeen years old, helped him. They organized the acquisition, storage and issue of supplies to the military.

Sheftal (1785-1797), who was born and raised in Savannah, was Chairman of the Savannah Parochial committee of resistance to British rule and was denounced and proscribed by the British.

He was able to acquire several hundred acres of land after the Revolution that were confiscated from the Loyalists as a reward for his efforts in the Revolution. The governor of Georgia wrote the British king, referring to the local Jews in the following:

"These people, my lord, were found to a man to be violent rebels and persecutors of your loyal subjects."

History books do not delve at all into Haym Salomon, though he was decidedly the best-known Jewish patriot. This was left to Jewish historians to elicit his deeds.

Salomon was Polish-born, came to the colonies at the age of 25 in 1740. He had traveled extensively throughout Europe and thus became fluent in German and French in addition to Polish. As a result he was employed by the British as an interpreter. Salomon was intimate with the Polish generals, Pulaski and Kosciuszko. He started out as a dry goods merchant but in 1776 he began an active involvement with the American cause. He was arrested as a spy by the British, presumably as a member of the Sons of Liberty organization, who planned to send fire ships into the harbor to destroy the British fleet. A modern guerrilla, you would call him today. He was even suspected of a part in a plot to burn the docks that the British used.

In prison, he was made an interpreter by the commander of the Hessian mercenaries who had been hired out by the king to fight the Americans. Salomon translated for the prisoners and guards. In 1777 he married Rachel Franks, daughter of a prominent merchant, Moses Franks, a common name at that time. Other prominent names were Levy, Abraham, and Lazarus. The last person was an ancestor to Emma Lazarus, who wrote the famous poem at the Statue of Liberty.

Give me your tired, your poor

Your huddled masses, yearning to be free

The wretched refuse of your teeming shore.

Send these, the homeless, tempest-tossed to me.

I lift my lamp beside the golden door!

(See her other unknown poem at the end of the chapter "Lincoln and the Jews")

While in prison, he helped prisoners escape and offered

them money. He was sentenced to death by the British as a spy, a sentence that was never carried out. I believe that he was a spy because he mentioned this in a letter of his to the Continental Congress. (The actual letter is at the end of this chapter.)

Had he been executed, the Jews might have had a martyr next to Nathan Hale, whom we all remember as the spy whose inscription on his statue reads *"I have but one life for my country."* Salomon escaped to Philadelphia leaving his wife and month-old child in New York. Now a fugitive from the British, Salomon lost no time in filing a petition with the Continental Congress in which he gave a detailed account of his efforts in behalf of the Revolution. Philadelphia at that time was also the patriotic capital, home of the Continental Congress, and had a prosperous Jewish community.

When Congress failed to act on his petition, he established himself and became eventually a very successful broker, negotiating contracts between buyers and sellers in all kinds of business. Although he had no capital, nor a supply of goods to sell, he had invaluable assets in his knowledge of markets and in the acquaintances he was making among Philadelphia businessmen. He was able to learn the market value of any commodity and many merchants came to rely on his information and expertise. His commodities included sugar, tea, even slaves, tobacco, hides, real estate, silk stockings, salt, dry goods and almonds. He even assisted in the exchange of the various monies that were separately issued by the various colonies. With this knowledge, he was made a treasurer for the French army, disbursing funds to the soldiers. He also exchanged European bills. Had he lived today, he may well have been a millionaire many times over, as he would have exchanged marks and yens for dollars with a great profit.

With his earned money, history indicates he helped some of the signers of the Constitution, charging very low interest rates. Most historians believe that it was a myth that he financed the Revolution. If anybody financed the Revolution, the French should be credited. They had a long history of antagonism towards the British. Remember Marquis de Lafayette, the famous Frenchman who helped the Americans. Salomon never claimed he lent money to the government. His son, years later, claimed he did. Salomon did lend money to delegates to the Continental Congress, like James Madison and Edmond Randolph, often charging no interest. This was due to the fact that the salary promised by the state of Virginia to its representative was being delayed and so they turned to Salomon for aid.

James Madison wrote the following to Edmond Randolph:

"The kindness of my little friend (Salomon) in Front Street will preserve me from extremities, but I never resort to it without mortification as he obstinately objects to any recompense. The price of money is so usurious that he thinks it ought to be extracted from none but those who aim at profitable speculations. To a necessitous delegate he gratuitously spares a supply out of his private stock." This was in September 30, 1782.

The success of Haym Salomon's brokerage enterprise, both in work for the Office of Finance and his private ventures, was due to Salomon's effective use of newspaper advertising. See page 9 for this advertising. He placed more than 1,050 ads in the short period between 1781 and 1785.

Salomon was one of many brokers working for Robert Morris, the Finance Minister, whom he asked for permission to use the title of broker to the Office of Finance. Morris's diary notes the following:

"This Broker has been useful to the public interest and requests leave to publish himself as a Broker to the office to which I have consented as I do not see that any disadvantage to the public service but the reverse and he expects individual benefits therefrom" —July 12, 1782.

Salomon took a strong stand on Jewish rights in the American community in Pennsylvania, which may well have influenced the eventual Bill of Rights of the US Constitution. He addressed the Pennsylvania Council of Censors, petitioning them to remove from the state constitution the Christian oath required of all office holders. He and other famous Jews of the time, such as Gershein Seixus, Barnard Gratz, and Simon Nathan wrote, *"Your memorilists apprehend with great submission that a clause in the Pennsylvania Constitution disables them to be elected by their fellow citizens to represent them in the Assembly is a stigma upon the nation and their religion and it is inconsonant with the second paragraph of the Pennsylvania Bill of Rights."* They all claimed they served in the Continental army and militia. The protest failed in 1783 but in 1790 the Pennsylvania state legislature became the first state to establish religious equality in politics.

A Quaker and Tory sympathizer used the assembly of Pennsylvania as a forum for a sensational denunciation of *"A Jew Broker"* slandering not only the Jewish religion and the Jewish people, but the livelihood and patriotism of the American Jews.

JEWISH PATRIOTS AND PIONEERS IN AMERICA

Isaac Pinto, Hebrew scholar, made his contribution to the culture of America with his translation of part of the daily and holiday prayer books into English from the original Hebrew. Appearing in 1766, this was not only the first work of its kind ever issued but the first book in English of a Jewish subject ever to be published in New York.

Isaac Pinto
(1721-1791)

The reply to this attack was made by Haym Salomon in Philadelphia's Independent Gazeteer, a newspaper at the time.

"You not only endeavored to injure me by your unwarrantable expressions but every person of the same religious persuasion I hold, and the laws of the country and the glorious toleration and liberty of conscience have allowed me to indulge and adopt.

I exult and glory in reflecting that we have the honor to reside in a free country."

Even at the 1787 Constitution Convention, the prohibition on religious tests for public office and the exclusion of reference to the Christian Deity, were not accepted. Some claimed that there should be at least some distinction between *"profession of Christianity and down right infidelity or paganism"* (the Jews).

When the various states were ratifying the Constitution, a delegate from North Carolina protested that *"in a political view, these gentlemen who formed the constitution should not have given this invitation to Jews and heathens."* Then it was asked by some whether it was possible to exclude anybody without taking away the principle of religious freedom.

It is most unfortunate that the Constitution Convention did not consider slavery. In fact, a member of the Virginia delegation refused to sign the Constitution because it refused to do away with slavery.

Throughout United States history, down to the present time, efforts have been proposed to have an amendment to the Constitution, that this nation is a Christian nation. Today, an amendment to the Constitution is being considered to allow prayer in the public schools. All this, in spite of the admonition of President Washington *"the government of the United States gives to bigotry no sanction, to prejudice, no assistance."*

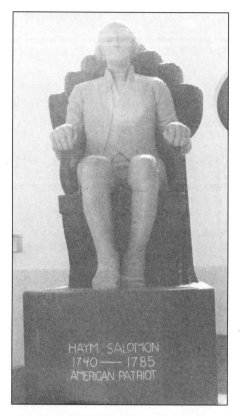

HAYM SALOMON
1740 —— 1785
AMERICAN PATRIOT

Statue of Haym Salomon in Los Angeles
Photo by Jewish Community Center of Los Angeles

The constant intervention of various Jewish organizations against assaults on religious freedoms demonstrates to all Americans the importance of the separation of church-state relations to American democracy in general.

There are two statues of Haym Salomon that exist in the country erected, not by the United States government, though many attempts in Congress were made to erect a statue. But it was up to the Polish Alliance of Chicago to erect a statue, which was dedicated on December 15, 1941, the 150th anniversary of the Bill of Rights. In this Chicago statue, we see George Washington in the center, surrounded by Robert Morris, the finance minister, and by Haym Salomon. The inscription on this Chicago statue reads as follows (refer to frontispiece):

"The government of the United States which gives to bigotry no sanction, to persecution no assistance, requires

See appendix D for complete Memorials.

(Name) Early ads began with list of goods and services (see opposite page). Moving name to top of ad helped enhance public recognition. With twenty-five brokers in town, personal reputation was important competitive edge.	**Haym Solomons,** BROKER to the Office of Finance, to the Consul General of France, and to the Treasurer of the French Army, at his Office in Front-street, between Market and Arch-streets, BUYS and SELLS on Commission	**(Broker to)** Reminded public of his role in the war effort. Used phrase "Broker to the Office of Finance" as though it were an official title, which it was not.
(Office in Front Street) Some late ads omit address altogether. Apparently, he was so well-established that location of his office was generally known.	**BANK** Stock, Bills of Exchange on France, Spain, Holland, and other parts of Europe, the West Indies, and inland bills, at the usual commission.——He Buys and Sells **Loan-Office Certificates,** Continental and State Money, of this or any other state, Paymaster and Quartermaster General's Notes; these and every other kind of paper transactions (bills of exchange excepted) he will charge his employers no more than ONE HALF PER CENT on his Commission.	**(Bank Stock Bills)** Primary business was trading in financial paper. Note variety of bills, bonds, and currencies.
(He receives) Dealt in wide range of commodities. Offered merchants advice on how and where to realize the best price for their goods.	**He procures Money on Loan** for a short time, and gets Notes and Bills discounted. Gentlemen and others, residing in this state, or any of the united states, by sending their orders to this Office, may depend on having their business transacted with as much fidelity and expedition, as if they were themselves present. He receives Tobacco, Sugars, Tea, and every other fort of Goods to Sell on Commission; for which purpose he has provided proper Stores.	**(One half per cent)** Specified low commission rate in ad
(Isaac Franks) Salomon's brother-in-law, and rival broker. The two competed in size and placement of ads throughout summer of 1782. Salomon's reference to work with Office of Finance was a coup his brother-in-law could not match.	**He flatters himself,** his assiduity, punctuality, and extensive connections in his business, as a Broker, is well established in various parts of Europe, and in the united states in particular. All persons who shall please to favour him with their business, may depend upon his utmost exertion for their interest, and—— Part of the Money advanced, if required. N. B. Paymaster-General's Notes taken as Cash for Bills of Exchange.	**(He flatters himself)** Recognized that success of his business depended on reliability of his services more than the nature of his merchandise. Despite boldness of his advertising, no claim he made has ever been shown to be false.

An advertisement of Haym Salomon in the local newspaper From the American Jewish Historical Society *only that they who live under its protection should demean themselves as good citizens, in giving it on all occasions their effective support."*

The inscription was taken from one of his letters to the new Rhode Island synagogue and is often referred to refute bigotry. He continued in this letter the following (the full letter is found at the end of this chapter).

"May the children of Abraham continue to merit and enjoy the good will of the other inhabitants while every one shall sit in safety under his own vine and there shall be none to make him afraid."

George Washington wrote a number of letters to various synagogues and one wonders why he wrote to such a small minority of the population who had no political power. I believe it is further confirmation of the Jewish role in the American Revolution. And today, in the United States, Jews have more political power than their numbers would indicate. They excel in many fields of endeavor.

There is also another statue of Haym Salomon in Los Angeles, California.

The Los Angeles statue of Haym Salomon
has the following inscription:
"1740-1785 American patriot: the human spirit has flowered only in freedom and the dynamic reality of our world culture flowed from its first democracy. Let all Americans acclaim Haym Salomon, a patriot, a benefactor of his country and an inciter to patriotism, to the members of his race, to his countrymen."

The complete dedication on erecting this statue is in Appendix D. A memorial postage stamp of Haym Salomon was issued in 1976 on the bicentennial of the Declaration of Independence. Many attempts in later years were made by his son to honor his memory but to no avail. Copy of the stamp, enlarged with both sides, is on the next page.

What kind of a man was Haym Salomon? He was a good father, husband, patriot, guerrilla and family man. Jewish

FINANCIAL HERO

Businessman and broker Haym Salomon was responsible for raising most of the money needed to finance the American Revolution and later to save the new nation from collapse.

historians who write about Salomon never mention or don't know his personal character. Perhaps, criticism may not be in the interests of the Jewish people. Other historians rarely take notice of Haym Salomon. Salomon did send money to his poor family in Poland and even provided a burial plot for them. His family, realizing he had money, tried to have him help them come to America. Here is part of a letter he sent to his uncle who was getting to annoy him.

"*Dear Uncle:*

Your bias of my riches are too extensive. Rich I am not but the little I have I think it is my duty to share with my father and mother. They are the first that are to be provided for by me and must and shall have the preference. Whatever little more I can squeeze out I will give my relations, but I tell you plainly and truly that it is not in my power to give you or any of my relations yearly allowances. D'ont you nor any of them expect it. D'ont fill your mind with vain and idol expectations — besides my mother and father, my wife and children must be provided for. I have three young children, and my wife is very young may have more.——but notwithstanding this I mean to assist my relations as far as lays in my power.

I am much surprised at your intention of coming here. Your yikes (family and academic background) is worth very little here; nor can I emagion what you mean to do here. I think your duty calls for your going to your family.

You are pleased to say you have done a great deal for my family. Let my father write me the particular services you have done to my family and I will consider in what manner to recompense them.

I desire no relation may be sent here. Have I not children, are they not relations? When I shall be fully informed of all young people in my family and their

qualifications explained, I may then perhaps advise send-
ing one or two to this country, and I will at my leisure
explain to you the nature of this country; VINIG
YIDISHKAYT (enough Jewishness).

Your affec'te nephew

Your very hum'e serv't

[Haym Salomon]"

This letter gives one a good idea of the personal image of Salomon. This letter of discouragement was accompanied by an order of six guineas. He previously had sent his uncle fifty guilders.

Salomon died on Jan. 6, 1785 at the age of 45, penniless, leaving a widow and four young children. While history indicates the exact date of his death, though, it is not known where he had been buried. I believe inflation made him insolvent. Inflation was known by other terms in those days. Salomon had to sell many of his securities at a fraction of his original cost due to the depression at that time. The executors of his estate (they had them at that time) found most of his holdings were in depreciated notes, and that his three children and pregnant wife, a twenty-three-year-old widow, were left not rich, but seriously in debt.

An obituary reporting Salomon's death was reported in many papers in New York, Philadelphia and Newport. This was considered at the time as an exceptional tribute because obituaries were infrequently printed.

Throughout the nineteenth and twentieth centuries there were attempts to honor and memorialize Haym Salomon in the halls of Congress but to no avail. Even President Taft tried to memorialize Salomon but nothing came of it. A US senator attempted to appropriate funds to Salomon's heirs as compensation for Salomon's deeds. This failed too.

Minorities, including the Jews and Afro-Americans, seek role models of their famous compatriots upon which they can base some of their actions and beliefs. It certainly enhances their status in their community. In many cases, it becomes a myth and this applies to Haym Salomon as the man who saved the American Revolution from collapse. This myth has been inculcated in many Jewish students. In fact, this is the only item they remember of the Jewish contribution to the Revolution. The myth may have been created to counter any anti-Semitism.

There were some Jews who opposed the Revolution because they found themselves in British-controlled areas like New York City and it was more convenient to remain than to leave. Loyalty was largely a function of location but the truth was that a clear majority, not necessarily Jews, did not support independence. They were more interested in the weather, price of coffee and real estate. John Adams had stated that one-third of the population was for the Revolution, one-third against and a third, neutral. Revolutions, worldwide, are often carried out by minorities of the population. Witness the French Revolution, Russian, Cuban and Chinese Revolutions.

Then, there were the Hessian soldiers, the German mercenaries, the Red Coates as they were often called, whom the British hired to fight the Americans. Some of these soldiers were Jews who wanted to get away from Germany. There were those Hessians that were captured by the British and forced to serve in the British army. A number of them became prominent in the Jewish community after the Revolution, one of whom was Abraham Zunz, an observant Jew, who was one of the founders of the New York Stock Exchange. He even became president of a congregation that had fled New York City. He was a native of Westphalia, arrived in 1779 and married a daughter of a well-known Jewish merchant and religious functionary. He had no difficulty in gaining the confidence of the Jewish community.

A Hessian soldier, familiar with traditional Jews in his native Germany, was surprised that the Jews he encountered in New York City were not bearded and that Jews did not hesitate to eat pork or consort with many gentiles. But if you were a member of a number of congregations in the US you were obligated to observe the dietary laws. In 1790 New York's congregation approved a bylaw that anyone who ate non-kosher food, or violated the Sabbath or any holiday would not be called to the Torah or receive any other religious honor in the synagogue, or be eligible for any congregational office. These congregations implicitly assumed that common religious observances and commonly shared religious values would bind them together as a community within the larger society. The congregations mandated sanctions for individuals who married out of the faith. I doubt if these sanctions were adhered to because there were many intermarriages. The paucity of Jews in the larger society could not avoid this problem in spite of the claim that any person who married contrary to religious law would be denied burial in the congregation's cemetery. Because this problem has existed for so long a movement is now trying to have the religious organizations welcome intermarriages since usually one of the couple, the female, kept the Jewish religion in spite of their Christian husbands.

The Loyalists were generally found among the rich merchants and the land owners who expected to benefit from their connection to Britain, some of whom fled to Canada. But after the war their land was confiscated and handed over to the eminent patriots.

An intellectual analysis for opposing the Revolution was made by a contemporary Jew, Isaac de Pinto (not to be confused with many Jewish named Pintos at that time). He was an economist and a publicist. He was not anti-American—he just opposed the Revolution and he made it quite known that he could not understand the reasons for opposing the King of England (he must have ignored the reasons in the Declaration of Independence). He claimed there was no ground for opposing the King of England as the British had been most generous to the colonies, supplying them with goods and services (usually at a higher price than elsewhere).

Isaac de Pinto even pleaded for a united Europe against the colonial revolt, suggesting they would lose trade if secession succeeded. He even implied that should the colonists succeed in the Revolution, they would expand to the Pacific and dominate most of the Americas—a true prediction, as witness the promulgation of the Monroe Doctrine in 1826 and subsequent events such as the Louisiana Purchase, the annexation of Texas after the Mexican War, and the annexation of many of the Indian lands. In later years they called this expansion the manifest destiny of the United States; others called it imperialism. Up until the Civil War most of the colonies had assumed that Canada would be part of the United States by conquest.

The British took up his writings for wide circulation throughout the colonies. Even Benjamin Franklin had to hire a Swiss publicist to refute de Pinto's writings. He wrote in his own publications, *"The Jew de Pinto whose venal pen has been employed in the most insolent manner against the Americans."* There is a myth that Benjamin Franklin may have been anti-Semitic but not so. He supported, liberally, the Congregation Mikveh Israel, Philadelphia. He was also associated with Benjamin Nones, a Jewish Revolutionary patriot.

In 1819, an historian, L. Shecut of Charlestown, S.C., paid tribute to the Jewish effort in the Revolution by writing, *"When the War of the Revolution commenced, all of the Jewish nation and able to bear arms, jealously joined in their country's martial ranks for the great but dubious contest."* This was written in his book or pamphlet *Topographical, historical, and other sketches of Charleston 1819.*

Jews in that era organized their synagogues, not only for religious reasons, but also to provide education for their children both in Hebrew and English. There were no public schools at that time—Jews were not discriminated in their personal and business lives—far less than their European counterparts. This may well be due to the Imperial Naturalization Act of 1740 in England that confirmed the status of the Jew to develop his talents as he saw fit. However, when it came to politics as previously mentioned, political oaths were common in spite of the Bill of Rights forbidding this discrimination. The Bill of Rights in that era did not apply to the states, only to the US government. The states were brought into the

Bill of Rights with the passage of the 14th Amendment to the Constitution in 1868. Part of this Amendment states, *"No state shall make or enforce any law which shall abridge the privileges or immunities of citizens of the United States nor shall any state deprive any person of life, liberty or property without due process of law, nor deny to any person within its jurisdiction the equal protection of the laws."*

We can see that the Jews did participate in many activities as patriots, not only in supplying commerce necessary for carrying out the war effort but also in money to the Americans. They fought as guerrillas in some cases, even spying as Haym Salomon proclaimed in his letter to the Continental Congress. Their presence may well have influenced the signers of the Bill of Rights, particularly in the separation of church and state in the First Amendment of the Bill of Rights. They are indeed the unrecognized patriots of the American Revolution. In some cases they were more important for their business and community accomplishments than for their military achievements.

In some respects, the American Revolution was a most important event in world Jewish history for it was the Revolution that was the basis for the mass migrations of the 19th and 20th centuries to the *"Goldenere Medina."*

The actual speech of President George Washington to the Rhode Island synagogue is as follows:

> *While I receive with much satisfaction your address replete with expressions of affection and esteem; I rejoice in the opportunity of assuring you I shall always retain a grateful remembrance of the cordial welcome I experienced in my visit to Newport from all classes of citizens.*
>
> *The reflections of the days of difficulty and danger which are past is rendered the more sweet from a consciousness that they are succeeded by days of uncommon prosperity and security. If we have the wisdom to make the best use of the advantages with which we are now favored we cannot fail, under the just administration of a good government to become a great and happy people.*

The citizens of the United States of America have a right to applaud themselves for having given to mankind examples of an enlarged and liberal policy, a policy worthy of imitation.

All possess alike liberty of conscience and immunities of citizenship. It is now no more that toleration is spoken of, as if it was by the indulgence of one class of people, that another enjoyed the exercise of their inherent natural rights. For happily the government of the United States, which gives to bigotry no sanction, to persecution no assistance, requires only that they who live under its protection should demean themselves as good citizens, in giving it on all occasions their effectual support.

It would be inconsistent with the frankness of my character not to avow that I am pleased with your favorable opinion of my administration, and fervent wishes for my felicity.

May the children of the stock of Abraham, who dwell in this land, continue to merit and enjoy the good will of the other inhabitants, while every one shall sit in safety under his own vine and fig tree, and there shall be none to make him afraid.

May the Father of all mercies scatter light and not darkness in our paths and make us all in our several vocations useful here, and in his own due time and way everlasting happy.

G. Washington

For other speeches of George Washington see Appendix B.

The actual letter of Haym Salomon to the Continental Congress is as follows:

The memorial of Haym Salomon late of the City of New York, merchant, humbly heweth, that your memorialist was some time before the entry of the British troops at the said City of New York, and soon after taken up as a spy and by General Robertson committed to the Provost—that by the interposition of Lieut. General

Heister who wanted him on account of his knowledge in the French, Polish, Russian Italian languages he was given over to the Hessian commander who appointed him in the commissary way as purveyor chiefly for the officers—that being at New York he has been of great service to the French and American prisoners and has assisted them with money and helped them off to make their escape—that this and his close connexions with such of the Hessian officer as were inclined to resign and with Monsieur Samuel Demezes has rendered him at last so obnoxious to the British headquarters that he was already pursued by the guards and Tuesday the 11th inst he made his escape from thence—this Monsieur Demezes is now most barbarously treated at the Provost's and is seemingly in danger of his life and the memorialist begs leave to cause him to be remembered to Congress for an exchange.

Your memorialist has upon this event most irrecoverably lost all his effects and credits to the amount of five or six thousand pounds sterling and left his distressed wife and child of a month old at New York waiting that they may soon have an opportunity to come out from thence with empty hands.

In these circumstances he most humbly prayeth to grant him any employ in the way of his business whereby he may be enabled to support himself and family—and your memorialist as in duty bound.

Phila Aug 25th 1778
Haym Salomon

He was denied any recompense.

Chapter II ───────────

Assimilation
1800-1860

There were a number of events in the early part of the nine-teenth century up to the Civil War era that need reporting. It was a time for the birth of Reform Judaism, beginnings of B'nai Brith and the influx of German Jews, such as Adam Gimbel, the future department store magnate. He came here at the age of 18 with no money and sold from farm to farm around Vincennes, Indiana. Edward Filene, who came from Poznan, Poland, began as a ped-dler, tailor and glazier. Lazarus Straus first peddled and then ran a country store. They peddled notions, dry goods, cheap jewelry and clothes. The Goldmans, Lehmans, Guggenheims, Seligmans and Werthams all shared a kind of collective biography.

In the plays, stories, books, and papers of the day, the Jew made his appearance as an untrustworthy peddler, as a greasy and filthy immigrant, as a dishonest, and a tax-avoiding businessman. The official organ of the Presbyterian Synod of New York, the

Missionary Record, denounced the Jews who had participated in the European republican uprisings of 1848 as destructive revolutionaries who had no real interest in the lands where they lived.

About 50,000 Jews left Central Europe between 1848 and 1860 to come to the United States. Had the Revolutions achieved political and economic opportunity for Jews, they might not have emigrated. Among the prominent Jews who emigrated at this time was August Bondi who joined John Brown's anti-slavery movement. Also arriving at this time was Michael Heilprin, who had been one of the propagandists for the Kossuth Hungarian Revolution and the one that denounced Rabbi Raphall for his

Courtesy of The Jewish Archives of America. Cincinnati, Ohio

An Early Jewish Peddler.

Rabbi Michael Heilprin

Courtesy of The Jewish Archives of America. Cincinnati, Ohio

Courtesy of The Jewish Archives of America. Cincinnati, Ohio

Rabbi Morris J. Raphall

attempt to prove that slavery had the sanction of the Jewish Bible. I believe the 1848 revolutions in Central Europe brought to the United States the greatest Jewish intellectuals of the time. Many of them became ardent supporters of the Republican party.

Even the highest ranking Jewish officer in the Civil War was Frederick Knefler, a product of these revolutions. Frederick Knefler (1833-1901) had served with Kossuth in Hungary at the age of 15 before moving to Indianapolis with his family. He volunteered with the Union army after Sumter and was commissioned a lieutenant. He was a Colonel of the 79th Indiana infantry by the time of the Chickamauga campaign in 1863. He was breveted a Brigadier General for gallant and meritorious service particularly at the Battle of Chickamauga Campaign. During that battle he led two Indiana regiments up the slope of Missionary Ridge, one of the most famous feats in all military history. Since he was part of the German intellectual movement he was antagonistic to all religions, believing that all obstacles between men should be broken down.

Knefler did not follow the Jewish religion and even intermarried.

Even today to quote from a study by Maurice and Marilyn Center for Modern Jewish Studies at Brandeis University revealed the *"synagogue least effective role is religious."* 43% of synagogue members surveyed *"believe belonging is very important while just 18% believe attending services is important."*

Jews in this era began to feel more and more that this is their land, that freedom of opportunity existed as nowhere else in the world, that their religion would not be an obstacle to a good life. They became acculturative to the Christian population. They wanted to reduce the differences between Judaism and Christianity and so the Reform movement started in 1824. They wanted a more rational means of worshipping their God, shortening the services and using English translations of the Hebrew. This still exists to this day in the United States. Many of them, particularly the native-born, were enlightened, cultured, thoroughly Americanized. Their minds had been set free by the American and French revolutions, and by the enlightenment. Many were unhappy with the inherited traditions of a largely Hebrew service and frequently objectional rituals. For most Jews and even to this day, religions remained important, the core of Jewish life and history, the only guarantee of continuity.

In July of 1820 in Savannah, Georgia a Synagogue was consecrated during which a Discourse was given by a famous doctor, Dr. Jacob De La Motta. He detailed the history of the Jews and their past persecutions throughout history and particularly the equality the Jews enjoyed in the United States compared to their brethren in other lands. He sent a copy of this discourse to President Madison and Thomas Jefferson, knowing their liberal views.

President Madison thanked Dr. De La Motta for sending him the discourse on the consecration of this new synagogue. He indicated that the history of the Jews must be forever interesting. He stated *"equal laws, protecting equal rights, are found, as they ought to be presumed, the best guarantee of loyalty and love of country; as well as best calculated to cherish that mutual respect and good will among citizens of* religious denominations which are necessary to social harmony, and most favorable to the advancement of truth. The account you give of the Jews in your congregation brings them fully in the scope of these observations."

Thomas Jefferson replied "I thank you for the discourse on the consecration of your synagogue in your city, with which you have been pleased to favor me. I have read it with pleasure and instruction, having learnt from it some valuable facts on Jewish history, which I did not know before. Your sect, by suffering, has furnished a remarkable proof of the universal spirit of religious intolerance in every sect, disclaimed by all while feeble and practiced by all when in power."

He continued "But more remains to be done, for although we are free by law, we are not so in practice. I salute you with great respect and esteem."

What a reply!! Can you imagine any of the potentates of Europe replying thusly.

It was the time when Jews appeared in a community where they purchased cemetery plots, organized mutual-aid benevolent societies and worshipped in private homes until there was enough money to rent a few rooms for a synagogue.

These years saw the establishment of a number of Jewish periodicals, mostly established in New York City. There was the *Occident* which happened to be the sole means of communication between the far-flung Jewish communities. Another periodical of the time was called the *Asmonean*.

Some of the tolerance towards Jews existed because many Christians felt the Jews can be ultimately converted to their religion. Organized American Christianity devoted many resources to this effort. All over the country programs were set up to attract Jews, particularly women and children. Evangelicals, despite their continuing failure, established themselves in storefronts in Jewish neighborhoods, roamed the streets looking for Jewish orphans and poor children and tried to get the courts to remand them to their care. They stalked charity wards of hospitals looking for dying Jews to make last-minute conversions. Apparently these converters considered their attempts to convert an act of kindness and charity. Perhaps the main source of interest in Judaism was sheer curiosity. There were few Americans who did not want to know more about these exotics whose faith was over 1000 years old and had survived all this persecution. After all it was the Jews who gave birth to Christianity. According to Jacob Marcus in his book *United States Jewry*, interest in Jews was also heightened by the thought that if the American Indians were the lost ten tribes, and if the restoration of the Jews was about to take place, then Jesus himself would speedily reappear.

Because of the ever-pervasiveness of anti-Semitism, an attempt was made, amongst others, to establish a tract of land in the United States in Mississippi and Missouri Territories. An association of wealthy and respectable Jews would be the prime movers. This would be an inducement for the Jewish population to enter agricultural pursuits. These facts would be published throughout Europe and become known to the Jews in the entire world. Thousands would flock to the land as proposed. Needless to say, no such statehood came to being in the American west. Later on a scheme to establish a Jewish state was proposed in Grand Island in New York but to no avail. All this was due to the fact that American Jews wanted to help their co-religionists around the world. This is further exemplified in the three notorious cases of anti-Semitism that occurred elsewhere.

In 1840, a Catholic priest and his servant in Damascus, Syria, disappeared. A rumor spread that they had been victims of Jews, killed so their blood could be baked into Passover matzo! The Ottoman governing bodies, eager to placate the Christian minority in the Empire, arrested several Jews, tortured them, sentenced many to death and indicated that up to thirty thousand were implicated. Jews all over the world protested to their governments, and demanded their governments use their diplomatic influence to relieve the Jews of Syria. This event may well have led to present Jews to indict further the current rulers of Syria for cruelty to Jews.

SKETCH

OF

PROCEEDINGS IN THE

Legislature of Maryland,

DECEMBER SESSION, 1818,

OR WHAT IS COMMONLY CALLED

The Jew Bill;

CONTAINING

THE REPORT OF THE COMMITTEE

APPOINTED BY THE HOUSE OF DELEGATES

To consider the justice and expediency of extending to those persons professing the Jewish Religion, the same privileges that are enjoyed by Christians:"

TOGETHER WITH

The Bill reported by the Committee,

AND

THE SPEECHES

OF

THOMAS KENNEDY, Esq. OF WASHINGTON COUNTY,

AND

H. M. BRACKENRIDGE, Esq. OF BALTIMORE CITY.

Baltimore:
PRINTED BY JOSEPH ROBINSON,
Circulating Library, corner of Market and Belvidere-streets.

1819

From the Jewish Archives

This is a replica of a Bill introduced in the Maryland Legislature to repeal the requirement to be a Christian in order to become a Legislator. It was repealed in 1827.

Another similar event occurred in 1858 with preposterous accusations.

In this case a young Jewish boy in Bologna, Edgar Mortara, had been abducted from his home by Vatican police after a Christian servant of the family told Catholic church authorities that she had him baptized, and therefore should not live in a Jewish family. This caused outrage for Jews all over the world, demanding their governments and in particular President Buchanan of the United States to intervene. He did not interfere, feeling that this would affect the US relations with foreign countries. The Jews at that time were not much of a political entity. The boy in the final analysis was not returned to his parents but it did lead to the rise of many Jewish organizations for more effective action in such matters. This activated political networks, lobbying government officials and stimulated the consciousness of Christians to the dangers faced by Jews in other lands.

Then there was the case of Captain Uriah P. Levy who was unjustly court-martialed in December, 1851, because he was a Jew.

Today, the US Navy officially recognizes Captain Uriah Phillip Levy as one of the heroes of American naval history. He lived from 1792 to 1862. In March, 1943, the navy launched a destroyer named after him. That he was discriminated against for more than 40 years, one writer in 1899 wrote designating Levy *"an American Dreyfus, forerunner of Dreyfus."*

It is unfortunate that history books in the United States have not recognized this naval hero. Perhaps had there been a great literary figure like Emile Zola of France in the United States, Levy would have been recognized similarly. Emile Zola defended Captain Dreyfus of France who was imprisoned for many years on an island in the Caribbean Sea, denied all privileges of an army officer, solely because he was a Jew.

Levy ran away from home in Philadelphia to serve as a cabin boy. At eighteen, he was already second mate of a brig and at twenty he was appointed a sailing master in the War of 1812. In 1817, he began his career as an officer in the United States navy when he was commissioned a lieutenant. He became a commander in 1837 and a captain in 1840.

Commander Levy was an admirer of Thomas Jefferson and donated a bronze statue of this President which now stands in

By Thomas Buchanan Read
Thomas Jefferson Read Reproduced in Portraits of Jews by Hannah London.
Courtesy of The Jewish Archives of America, Cincinnati, Ohio

Commodore Uriah P. Levy

statuary hall in the Capitol in Washington, DC. He had commissioned this statue from a famous sculptor in France. For many years he was the owner of Thomas Jefferson's home in Monticello which he bought for $27,000. Levy's fortune was made in New York real estate of which it was estimated in 1846 to be $250,000.

Uriah P. Levy died in New York in 1862 and is buried in Cypress Hills Cemetery on Long Island. He offered his entire fortune to President Lincoln for his country's use. Commodore Levy's name is memorialized in the Jewish Chapel on the Norfolk Naval Base by naming it the Commordore P. Levy Chapel.

He did not like flogging in the navy as a punishment for any violation of navy rules. Levy was instrumental in abolishing this antiquated form of punishment. No mention in naval history is this event ever noticed. As a Jew he faced ostracism, insults, and six court martials in which he was always found guilty and given excessive punishment. He was even dismissed from the navy but surprisingly, he persevered and was finally vindicated by a powerful defense. A defense which can be appropriate in similar cases of anti-Semitism today.

Some excerpts of his defense before the court of inquiry, December 18, 1857 are quoted herein:

"My parents were Israelites. I was nurtured in the faith of my ancestors. In deciding to adhere to it I have but exercised a right guaranteed by the Constitution of my state and of the United States. I never failed to acknowledge and respect like freedom in others. From the time I aspired to a lieutenancy and still more and after I gained it I was forced to endure a large share of the prejudice and hostility for which for so many ages the Jews have been persecuted.

This is the case before you. It is the case of every Israelite in the Union. I need not speak to you of their number. They are unsurpassed by any portion of our people in loyalty to the Constitution and to the union; in their quiet obedience to the laws; and in the cheerfulness with which they contribute to the public burdens. Many of them have been distinguished by their liberal donations to the general interests of education and of charity.

And of my brethren in this land and as well as those of foreign birth as of American descent—how rarely does any one of them become a charge controlled by Christians. How largely do they all contribute to the activities of trade; to the interests of commerce; to the stock of public welfare! Are all these to be proscribed? Is this the language to be spoken to the ear but broken in the hope, of my race. Are the thousands of Israelites in their dispersions throughout the earth, who look to America a land of bright with promise—are they now to learn to their sorrow and dismay; that we too have sunk into the mire of religious intolerance and bigotry? And are the American Christians now to begin the persecution of the Jews?

And think not if you once enter on this career it can be limited to a Jew. What is my case today if you yield to this injustice may tomorrow be that of a Roman Catholic or the Unitarian, the Episcopalian or the Methodist. Perhaps the Austrian priest, Niemoller, during World War II uttered the same thoughts during the Nazi terror, which statement made history at the time."

See appendix C for complete speech.

Uriah Levy, who was so proud of his part in the agitation against flogging in the American navy, was not an abolitionist when slavery was under discussion. He kept slaves on his Virginia plantation.

Jews feared to emigrate in the early part of the nineteenth century—it was a vast unknown—transportation was hazardous and not much was known about the Jews in America. Then there was a decline in piety at this time as previously noted. One rabbi noted *"the religious life in this land is at the lowest level—most people eat forbidden fruit and desecrate the Sabbath in public."* It was not like this in the later part of the nineteenth century when the great migrations occurred from eastern Europe. It has been estimated that about 35 million Jews arrived in those times.

A popular nineteenth-century joke that made the rounds of the population involved a simple cowboy who had just left a camp meeting. Upon seeing a Jew, he struck him down forcefully. The bewildered peddler, or shopkeeper, asked what he had done to incur such an attack, and the Christian replied, *"You crucified our Lord."* When the Jew explained that the event had taken place eighteen hundred years earlier, the ignoramus thought that it had happened recently and begged the Jew's pardon.

In spite of many anti-Semitic actions by the press and others, many gentiles did not wish to subject Jews to disabilities because of their religious convictions. The government of the United States did believe in tolerance for different religions. Here and there, individuals adhered to the belief that all religions must be equal before the law.

The Mexican war in which Jews participated was an unpopular war. Many in Congress and the anti-slavery forces felt it was unjust, aggressive and created by the president to enlarge the areas in which slaves can pick cotton. Even Abraham Lincoln, then a Congressman, opposed the war. For these reasons many Jews did not participate in this war—it was a volunteer war on the part of the soldiers.

In summary, Jews in this era were mostly in mercantile endeavors, particularly clothing. There were few professionals and less farmers. The Jew was an independent merchant. Labor was not organized. It had to wait until 1881 when Samuel Gompers started the American Federation of Labor. Jews were more employers proportionately than other Americans. Many Jews became prosperous such as the Sterns, Kuhns, Seligmans and the Rothschilds, but not as much as the Morgans, the Drexels and the Rockefellers. Living conditions in the cities such as New York were difficult. Toilets were in the yards and water was obtained from a common hydrant in the yard.

Chapter III _____

Lincoln and the Jews

I do not like to hear a class or nationality condemned on account of a few sinners.   *A. Lincoln*

To what extent was Abraham Lincoln favorable to Jewish causes? To what extent did the Jews participate in the Civil War? Was President Lincoln a friend of the Jewish people? These issues will be discussed in the following pages.

Anti-Semitism was an issue, at times, during the Civil War—a case of class action against the entire Jewish community.

On October 25, 1862 General Ulysses S. Grant assumed command of the operations in the state of Mississippi and Tennessee. One of his problems was to limit the trade with the Confederacy. Speculators swarmed into these states to profiteer, at great profits. Some were Jewish merchants—Grant, however, identified the entire traffic with the Jews as such! He issued specific orders to forbid travel in the area under his control especially to the *"Israelites especially"* because they were *"such intolerable nuisance."* Grant issued his General Order No. 11 as follows:

"The Jews, as a class, violating every regulation, of trade established by the Treasury Department are hereby expelled from these territories within twenty four hours of receipt of this order."

He omitted all others from this general order—only the Jews. He refused to recognize that the business traffic and speculation were being conducted by all religious groups including officers in his own command. Nevertheless, he singled out the Jewish merchants for punishment. The classic case of racism—blaming the many for the wrongs of the few.

Almost immediately, the Jewish community protested the harsh policy. A letter by Mr. S. Wolf and brothers, the unofficial representative of American Jewry, wrote to the President *"the undersigned, good and loyal citizens for the United States engaged in legitimate*

Hon. Simon Wolf.

Reproduced from History of the Jews in America by Peter Wiernik (1912)
Courtesy of The Jewish Archives of America, Cincinnati, Ohio

business as merchants, feel greatly insulted and outraged by this inhuman order, the carrying out of which would be a gross violation of the Constitution and our rights as citizens under it, and would place us, besides a large number of other Jewish families of this town, as outlaws before the whole world. We, respectfully, ask your immediate attention to this enormous outrage of all laws and humanity and pray for your effectual and immediate interposition."

President Lincoln was surprised that General Grant could have issued such a ridiculous and absurd order and added *"to condemn a class, is to say the least, to wrong the good with the bad. I do not like to hear a class or nationality condemned on account of a few sinners."*

Lincoln, at once, had his military advisor, General Halleck, write General Grant that the President had no objection to expelling traitors, profiteers, and some Jewish peddlers, but in terms proscribed for an entire religious class, some of whom are fighting in our ranks, the President deemed it necessary to revoke the order of General Grant No. 11.

With a single firm directive, President Lincoln put an end to the first anti-Semitic act of the government of the United States.

This action on the part of the President showed he knew of no distinction between Jew and Gentile, that he felt no prejudice against any nationality and that he by no means will allow a citizen in any wise be wronged on account of his place of birth or religious status.

During General Grant's presidency he apologized to the Jews for this action. In fact, he offered a Cabinet post to a Jew, Joseph Seligman, who declined the offer. Further, during the pogroms in 1870 in Rumania, Grant performed a major service to the Jews of the world. He appointed a Grand Master, Benjamin Plexott of the B'nai Brith organization that defends human rights and fights discrimination throughout the world, to serve as a consul at Bucharest in an effort to bring pressure on the Rumanian government to stop the attacks on the Jews.

General Grant wrote a letter to a Congressman, I.N. Morris of Illinois, in which he attempted to make it appear that the order was written in a moment of spontaneous anger, and that it would not have received his sanction if he had taken time to consider its implications. The letter in part read as follows:

"I have no prejudice against any sect or race, but want each individual to be judged on his own merit. Order No. 11 does not sustain this statement, I admit, but then I do not sustain that order. It would never have been issued if it had not been telegraphed the moment it was penned, and without reflection."

In an interview which President Grant gave to Rabbi E.B. Browne of Long Branch, New Jersey on August 27, 1875, he said in part, *"I have found Jewish soldiers, amongst the bravest of the brave. The Jew risks his life only to show his patriotism, and then he is fearless. The Jewish soldiers, as stated, I have found to be wonderfully courageous in our army and in the rebel lines as well————I have appointed more Jews than any of my predecessors."*

Bertram Korn, the author, writes that only by recognizing the fact that some persons are the victims of unconscious prejudices—that men sometimes assimilate stereotyped images, bigoted ideas from their environment of which they are utterly unaware and which lie dormant until called forth by some severe experience. I believe this to be true and that General Grant was not anti-Semitic. I believe that this psychology of Bertram Korn can be applied to many modern aspersions of racism.

Lincoln had a number of Jews as confidantes, similar to Harry Hopkins in President Roosevelt's administration, one a chiropodist, Isachar Zacharie, who operated on Lincoln's feet. Lincoln sent him on a number of missions to the Confederacy for possible peace overtures. Zacharie worked zealously for Lincoln's election in 1864. He traveled throughout New York and Pennsylvania speaking at rallies for the Republican party. In a report to the White House he wrote *"as regard the Israelites with but few exceptions, will vote for you and have taken precaution that they do as promised."* I believe that he advised Jews to vote against candidates who approved a Constitutional amendment recognizing Christianity as the official religion of the country. The same agitation for a similar amendment to the Constitution appears to be in vogue currently. Dr. Zacherie, the chiropodist, even addressed the President as *"my dear friend."*

The New York World at that time wrote *"the President has often left his business apartment to spend an evening in the parlor with this favored bunionist."* Lincoln often discussed with him high matters of state policy. After Lincoln's death he became unknown, returned to his native England where he died in 1897.

Another Jew, a personal friend of Lincoln, was Abraham Jonas, who arrived from England in 1819 and had come to Cincinnati, Ohio. He became friendly with Lincoln in 1838 because they had been together in politics. He had spent four terms in the Kentucky House of Representatives and Lincoln had spent two terms in the Illinois House. Jonas was a very successful Jew where there were few Jews around. He became a lawyer and good debater, which helped Lincoln later on.

In 1854 he became very close to Lincoln and had invited Lincoln to Quincy, Illinois to speak before the Whig party in behalf of a friend of Jonas's who was seeking a seat in the US Congress. When Stephen Douglas, the great debater, was going to speak for the Democratic candidate, Jonas had felt a reply by Lincoln to Douglas would be more effective than any other person.

In December of the same year of 1854 Jonas was doing a lot of political work for Lincoln. I believe he was quite helpful in obtaining the nomination of Lincoln in 1860 for the Presidential candidate of the Republican party.

Lincoln allowed, on one occasion, the son of Jonas, a Confederate soldier who was then a Union prisoner, to visit his dying father. Lincoln issued the following telegram: *"Allow Charles H. Jonas, now a prisoner of war at Johnson Island, a parole of 3 weeks to visit his dying father, Abraham Jonas, at Quincy Illinois. June 17, 1864."*

After Lincoln's election, Jonas had reliably found out that

Abraham Jonas

First person in the United States to mention Lincoln as a candidate for the presidency. He was a personal friend of Lincoln. In his capacity of County Chairman of the Republican Party in Quincy, Ill., he arranged a special conference, attended by Horace Greeley, at which Lincoln's name was broached. Jonas was Grand Master of Masons of the Grand Lodge of the State of Kentucky, and subsequently Grand Master of the Grand Lodge of the State of Illinois.

some prominent Southerners were plotting to assassinate the President. He pleaded with him to take all precautions and sure enough, a few months later, Lincoln arrived in Washington under secret guard to avoid any threatened attack on him. At that time Presidents were not protected as they are today. Too bad Lincoln was not protected similarly in the Ford Theatre on April 14, 1865! The saying went at that unfortunate time that had he been a Jew or Catholic he would have been in synagogue or church instead of that eventful theatre. Maybe!

For continuing friendship with Abraham Jonas, Lincoln appointed the wife of Jonas to fill out the unexpired term of Quincy, Illinois postmistress, thus paying another tribute to his friendship to his comrade who had shared many principles and interests and who had been loyal to him.

There were extensive letters between the President and these two Jewish people. In fact, the White House was practically open to them. Lincoln believed in their integrity to discuss high matters of state policy.

Here are some excerpts of a letter sent to President Lincoln from I. Zacharie MD:

To His Excellency
 A. Lincoln

 Washington DC

> *760 Broadway*
> *New York Nov 3 1859*

My dear friend,

> *I just returned to this city after a trip of 9 days through Pennsylvania and New York states, and I am happy to inform you, that I am satisfied that I have done much good. I now think all is right—and if I can reduce the Democratic majority in this city, I shall be satisfied. As regards the Israelites, with but few exceptions, they*

will vote for you. I understand them well and have taken the precaution, to see that they do as they promised. I have secured good and trustworthy men to attend to them on Election Day. My men have been all the week seeing that their masses are properly registered. So that all will be right on the 8th ins.

As regards Pennsylvania, if you knew all—you and your friends would give me much credit, for I flatter myself I have done the sharpest things that has been done in the campaign. Will explain to you when I see you.

With regards to Mrs Lincoln

Yours truly,
I. Zacharie

Executive Mansion

Hon Secretary of War
Washington DC Jan 25, 1865

My dear sir

About Jews, I wish you would give Dr. Zacharie a pass to go to Savannah, remain a week and return, bringing him, if he wishes his father and sisters or any of them. This will spare me the trouble and oblidge me—I promised him long ago that he should be allowed this whenever Savannah should fall into our hands.

Yours truly,
A. Lincoln

Dr. Zacharie's family had lived there all during the war and President Lincoln by this letter afforded Dr. Zacharie the first opportunity to visit his family.

Dr. Zacharie helped many New Orleans and Confederate Jews with their many problems, for which he was given a testimonial. At this testimonial he said, *"Let us look at England, France, Russia, and, almost every nation in the world, and where do we find the*

Israelite, we find them taken into the confidence of kings and emperors."

Lincoln liked Dr. Zacharie even though he had no political following, was an unimportant foreigner, but he believed in his integrity to discuss high policies of government and permitted almost free access to his office.

Lincoln said this of Dr. Zacharie: *"I myself have high regards for the Jews, my chiropodist is a Jew, and he has so many times put me upon my feet that I have no objection to giving his countrymen a leg up."*

Simon Wolf, unofficial Jewish representative to Republican presidents, and a most prominent citizen, was successful in his effort to acquire a pardon for a Jewish deserter. A Jewish soldier was to be executed at sunrise the next morning. The young man had been refused a furlough to visit his dying mother. He was overcome with grief that he deserted his post and was subsequently arrested, tried and condemned to be shot. After pulling some strings with influential politicians, Mr. Wolf managed to get an interview with President Lincoln at 2 AM. He got the President out of bed since the execution was to take place that morning.

At first, the President refused to do anything about this because he had already pardoned too many, according to Secretary of State Stanton. Mr. Wolf informed him that he never granted a pardon to a Jewish soldier. Lincoln agreed to stop the execution. He had the quality of *"rachmonos"*—the quality of mercy—in a large measure.

Months after, the soldier Lincoln had saved was killed in action at the Battle of Cold Harbor. When informed of this, Lincoln became visibly moved and with great emotion said, *"Thank God for having done what I did."*

One of the quaintest stories Simon Wolf tells is this:

One day I received a letter from a Jew in Jerusalem, who wrote me in jargon (yiddish), which Henry Gersony, lately deceased, managed to decipher, and the request was that I should see the "King of the United States" and bring to his attention the fact *that he, the Jew of Jerusalem, had a daughter whom he wished to be married, and he wanted to do the "king of the United States" the honor to have him contribute to her dowry. The request was so amusing that I stated it to the President, and he said, "Do you think this man is in ernest?" and I said, "None more so," and he promptly gave me a check for $25 which I forwarded to my correspondent. Subsequently I received a letter of thanks in Hebrew, also the portrait of General Grant in Hebrew letters, which I believe, will be found among the other Grant treasures on exhibition in the National Museum.*

At the beginning of the Civil War there were no provisions for a Jewish chaplain. The law provided for a chaplain *"who must be a regular ordained minister of some Christian denomination."* Estimates of the number of the Jewish soldiers were about 5000 in a total Jewish population of 150,000.

The Jews at that time felt that a chaplain who had to be *"of a Christian denomination"* would be the first step towards their exclusion from other public office. They also claimed that this exclusion may be applied for the oppression of other religious societies. A representative of the Board of Delegates of American Israelites, the Rev. Arnold Fischel appeared at the White House and the President received him cordially. Rev. Fischel told the President he had not come to seek any political office but *"to contend for the principle of religious liberty and for the welfare of the Jewish volunteers."* President Lincoln did not think that the Congress had intentionally omitted the exclusion of Jewish chaplains. The President claimed that this was the first time he had heard about this subject. A few days later, Rev. Fischel received the following letter from President Lincoln:

Rev. Dr. A. Fischel

My Dear Sir:

I find there are several particulars in which the present law in regards to chaplains is supposed to be defi-

cient, all which I now design presenting to the appropriate committee of Congress, I shall try to have a new law broad enough to cover what is desired by you in behalf of the Israelites.

Yours truly,
A. Lincoln

The law to exclude Jewish chaplains was overturned to include rabbis and thereupon President Lincoln appointed Rabbi Joseph Frankel of Philadelphia as the first Jewish chaplain.

Interestingly, in the Confederacy the equality of the chaplains was recognized immediately upon the outbreak of the war. There were no denominational specifications, to exclude Jewish chaplains. But there was no request to have one.

At one time the President had thought of a Jewish state in Palestine being worthy of consideration as a result of a suggestion of a prominent Zionist at the time. However, it was no time for such consideration with the war going on.

When Lincoln's son Willie died, a prayer was held in Mikveh Israel Synagogue, Philadelphia:

"Bless the President of the United States; bless him for his sterling honesty; bless him for his firmness and moderation."

A copy of the full prayer was sent to President Lincoln, who acknowledged its receipt. A facsimile of this reply is on the next page.

Some Jewish women in the South helped the Confederacy, sewing uniforms, nursing the wounded, some disguised themselves as men and fought in the Confederate army. Eugenie Phillips, a Jewess, became a spy for the Confederate army. They would pass on vital information on the whereabouts of the Union army. She was accused of teaching her children to spit on officers of the Union army. For this she was imprisoned for months. Her husband, Philip Phillips, was an outstanding attorney in the South

Facsimile of Lincoln's letter to A. Hart, President of
Mikveh Israel congregation, Philadelphia.

and had served in the House of Representatives. He was known as
a strong opponent of the Know Nothing party, who opposed the
entry of Jews into the country as well as others. Lincoln once said,
"When the Know Nothing party get control, they will declare all
men are equal except Negroes, Catholics and foreigners. When it
comes to this I shall prefer emigrating to some country where they
make no pretense of loving liberty such as Russia."

Lincoln met many prominent Jews during his administration, which really broadened his experience with the Jewish people.

When news of Lincoln's assassination reached synagogues, black draperies were quickly hung on the altars—Yom Kippur hymns and chants were substituted for Passover melodies.

Rabbi Isaac sermonized, *"The lamented Abraham Lincoln believed himself to be bone from our bone and flesh. He supposed himself to be a descendant of Hebrew parentage. He said so in my presence."* I doubt the veracity of his statement. Allow me to quote the final paragraph of a funeral oration by Dr. Max Lilienthal at the Broadway Synagogue in Cincinnati, April 19, 1865:

"We will stand firm to our government and our flag, till the work thou has so gloriously begun shall be brought to a still more glorious end. Smile on! They can not bury the principles thou has bequeathed us; thy name shall be as immortal as the truth of thy teaching. Abraham Lincoln, friend of the people, the poor and the slave, farewell! We will cherish and revere thy memory forever; for thou was great, because thou was good. Farewell, till God grants us a meeting in eternity."

There probably was no synagogue in the North that did not conduct services or cantor that did not deliver a sermon on Lincoln's death. In fact, a book was published in 1927 by Hersh and Block Publishing Co. to record all the tributes to Lincoln upon his death. The title of this book was *"Lincoln, A Tribute Of The Synagogue."* I have quoted from this book. A monument association was formed by leading Jews to contribute for a monument, this book, to the memory of Lincoln. It was requested from many Jews to prove themselves patriotic citizens as well as reverence for Lincoln's memory. So American Jewry paid a last tribute to the President who had appointed the first Jewish chaplain and remanded the most anti-Semitic regulation in American history.

I believe had Lincoln lived much of the racism that followed the Civil War would not have occurred for it is interesting to note that the Klu Klux Klan was organized in 1866. He had often urged his countrymen to abandon all thoughts of vengeance against the foes who had embroiled them in a four-year-long holocaust. Northern Republicans treated the south with a ferocity that was alien to Lincoln. Southern legislators enacted the infamous Black Codes which restored much of slavery in all but name.

Jews, as a result of the Civil War and Lincoln's beneficence, learned the importance of petitioning, of organizing societies and institutions. They realized the importance of American safeguards of the rights of religious minorities.

Four Jews attained the rank of General Officer in the Union army, and two Jews, Sgt. Leopold Karpeles and Abraham Cohen, of the 68th New York Volunteers in 1864, won the Congressional Medals of Honor. It was given for *"conspicuous gallantry displayed, in the Battle of the Wilderness in rallying and reforming disorganized troops under heavy firing."* From official statistics, a Major General O.O. Howard, not a Jew, speaks of one of his Jewish staff officers as being *"of the bravest and best"*; of another—killed at Chanceville—as *"being a true friend and a brave officer."* He continues, *"Intrinsically there are no more patriotic men to be found in this country than those who claim to be of Hebrew descent, and who served with me in parallel commands or more directly under my instructions."*

During the Civil War there was an increase in anti-Semitism over the days of the Revolution because of the increase in immigration and I believe in the increase of the popularity of the Know Nothing party who opposed immigration and other minorities. Lincoln, as mentioned previously, fought this party. We have the same situation regarding immigration at the present time. There was a clamor to eliminate immigration, deny basic medical benefits to new immigrants and even possibly repudiating their basic civil rights. So it is today!

Typical of the anti-Semitic remarks at that time are the following:

"Foreign Jews were scattered all over the country, under official protection, engaged in trade to the exclusion of our own citizens, undermining our currency."

"Jews participated in every aspect and process of the exploitation of the defenseless blacks."

"The Jews seem to be a privileged class that can travel anywhere."

"War time inflation and scarcity are due to Jewish extortioners and speculators. They were in league with the Confederate quartermaster General Myers, a Jew."

John Beauchamp Jones, attached to the Confederate War Department, wrote in his diary of 1862:

"These Jews have injured the cause more than the armies of Lincoln. Well, if we gain our independence, instead of being the vassals of the Yankees we shall find all our wealth in the hands of the Jews."

"The illicit trade with the United States has depleted the country of gold and placed us at the feet of the Jew extorters. These Jews have injured the cause more than the armies of Lincoln."

One more amazing diatribe.

"Otto Von Bismarck, German chancellor (1871-90) wrote the following:

It is not to be doubted, I know of absolute certainty, that the division of the United States into two federations of equal power had been decided upon well in advance of the Civil War by the top financial powers of Europe. These bankers were afraid that the United States, if they were to remain one and were developed into one nation only would achieve economic and financial independence, and this later would completely upset the capital domination of Europe over the world.

Of course, within the 'inner circle' of finance, the voice of the Rothchilds dominated. They foresaw the chance of prodigious booty if they could substitute two weak democracies, burdened with a debt, imploring the aid of Jewish financiers, in place of the vigorous Republic, confident and proud, sufficient unto herself. Consequently, they put their emissaries in the field to exploit the question of slavery, to open up the abyss between the two sections of the Union———The rupture between the North and South became inevitable; the masters of European Finance employed all the forces at their disposal in bringing it about and to turn it to their account."

Some of the above statements, particularly the statement of Von Bismarck, was taken from an unknown anti-Semite who sent these *"facts"* to me when I wrote an article on Lincoln and the Jews in the Jewish Voice of the Jewish Federation of Monmouth County, New Jersey. His heading was "Yankees weren't the only enemies of the South."

Such was the Judiophobia at that time.

It is the Jewish Encyclopedia, 1986, there was the report of General Butler, a Northern general who announced the capture of 150 Rebels, 90 mules, 60 contraband and five Jews. Lincoln thought this was a joke but it wasn't funny to the Jews.

I found this quotation from a speech of Mr. Lincoln in July 1958, in Chicago:

"Let us discard all this quibbling about this man and the other man, this race and that race, and the other race being inferior and therefore they must be placed in an inferior position. Let us discard all these things and be united as one people throughout the land, until we shall once more stand up declaring that all men are created equal." Could this statement be applied to our modern times!

It would be appropriate to quote the famous Gettysburg address, to show the greatness of this President, the most popular of all presidents (5000 volumes have been printed on him alone and more coming) and a friend of the Jewish people.

Fourscore and seven years ago our fathers brought forth on this continent a new nation, conceived in liberty and dedicated to the proposition that all men are created equal.

Now we are engaged in a great civil war, testing whether this nation or any nation so conceived and so dedicated can long endure. We are met on the great battlefield of that war. We have come to dedicate a portion of that field, as a final resting place for those who here gave their lives that that nation might live. It is altogether fitting and proper that we should do this.

But in a larger sense, we can not dedicate—we can not consecrate—this ground. The brave men, living and dead, who struggled here, have consecrated it, far above our poor power to add or detract. The world will little note, nor long remember, what we say here. It is for us the living, rather, to be dedicated here to the unfinished work, which they who fought here have thus far so nobly advanced. It is rather for us to be here dedicated to the great task remaining before us—that from these honored dead we take increased devotion to that cause for which they gave their last full measure of devotion—that we highly resolve that these dead shall not have died in vain—that this nation, under God, shall have a new birth of freedom—and that government of the people, by the people, for the people, shall not perish from the earth.

Because of this address some historians state we live in a different America. It determines how we read the Declaration of Independence.

There were some harsh criticisms of this Gettysburg Address notably from the Chicago Times who quoted the letter of the Constitution to Lincoln noting the lack of reference to equality, its adherence to slavery, and said that Lincoln was betraying the instrument he was called to defend. How dare he, the Times

Their New Jerusalem

The only one left on Broadway

APRIL 27, EIGHTEEN-SIXTY-FIVE

By EMMA LAZARUS

THE flight, pursuit, and remorse of Lincoln's assassin have been vividly portrayed by Emma Lazarus in a poem herewith appended. She chose for her title the date of Booth's capture and death, inadvertently giving it a day too late. These verses first appeared in 1867, in "Poems and Translations by Emma Lazarus, Written between The Ages of Fourteen and Seventeen." Owing to their ambiguous title their existence has escaped the notice of most students of Lincoln.

"Oh, where can I lay my aching head?"
The weary-worn fugitive sadly said.
"I have wandered in all the sleepless night,
And I saw my pursuers distant light
As it glared o'er the river's waves of blue,
And flashed forth again in each drop of dew—
I've wandered all night in this deadly air,
Till, sick'ning, I drop with pain and despair."

Go forth! Thou shalt have here no rest again,
For thy brow is marked with the brand of Cain.

"I am weary and faint and ill," said he,
"And the stars look down so mercilessly!
Do you mock me with your glittering ray,
And seek, like the garish sun, to betray?
Oh, forbear, cruel stars, so bright and high;
Ye are happy and pure in God's own sky.
Oh, where can I lay me down to sleep,
To rest and to slumber, to pray and weep?"

From the book A. Lincoln— The Tribute of the Synagogue by Hertz, Block Publishing Co. 1927

THE TRIBUTE OF THE SYNAGOGUE

Go forth! Thou shalt have here no rest again,
For thy brow is marked with the brand of Cain.

"To sleep! What is sleep now but haunting dreams?
Chased off, everytime by the flashing gleam
Of the light o'er the stream of yonder town,
Where all are searching and hunting me down!
Oh, the wearisome pain, the dread suspense,
And the horror each instant more intense!
I yearn for the rest from my pain and for sleep—
Bright stars, do ye mock, or quivering, weep?"

Go forth! Thou shalt have here no rest again,
For thy brow is marked with the brand of Cain.

On the marsh's grass, without pillow or bed,
Fell the rain and dew on his fated head;
While the will-o'-the wisp with its changeful light,
Led him on o'er the swamp in the darksome night;
And all Nature's voices cried out again,
To the weary fugitive in his pain—

Go forth! Thou shalt have here no rest again,
For thy brow is marked with the brand of Cain.

The pursuers are near! Oh, bitter strife!
Youth, more strong than despair still clings to life.
More near and more near! They find him at last;
One desperate struggle, and all is past—
One desperate struggle, mid smoke and flame,
For life without joy, and darkness and shame.
A prayer ascends to high Heaven's gate
For his soul, O God, be it not too late!
A ball cleaves the air. . . . He is lying there,
Pale, stiff and cold in the fresh morning air;
And the flames' hot breath is all stifled now,
And the breezes caress his marble brow.

All sorrow has gone with life's fitful breath.
Rest at last! For thy brow bears the seal of death.

continued, then standing on the graves at Gettysburg mistake the cause for which they died. They were men possessed of too much respect to declare that negroes were their equals or were entitled to equal privileges.

Another letter of I. Zacharie to President Lincoln.

To his
Excellency A. Lincoln   *St. Charles Hotel*
President of United States   *New Orleans, April 25th, 1863*
Washington, D.C.

Dear Sir,

After an absence of five weeks I find but little change in the condition of affairs in this city. The levee and some parts of the business district are less lively. This is to be accounted for in the decreased receipt of produce. The Crop of sugar within our lines has been brought to market and disposed of. The Crop of cotton in Southern Lousiana has never been much of importance. The high prices ruling in January, February and March brought every bale to market. Thus the planter having disposed of his produce we cannot look for a revival of business until the country now regained by Gen. Banks throws off its shackles and is again opened to the commercial world.

As regards the feelings of the people—which I have given much attention to—I find the kind disposition evinced towards Gen. Banks continues. There are a few who will complain, but the feeling towards yourself and the general Government is improving. The Union associations of the city have five thousand names enrolled, & there are many good Union men here who have not yet enrolled

The recent rapid and effective movements of the army under the leadership of the General commanding in person, has given courage, new life as it were, to all true lovers of the Union, while its enemies, it has astonished and disheartened. The country regained is the finest portion of the State, & the people there yield submissively to

Abraham Cohen
68th N.Y. Volunteers recipient of Medal of Honor in the Civil War

Emma Lazarus (1849-1887)
U.S. poet and essayist. The base of the Statue of Liberty in New York Harbor bears the lines of Emma Lazarus' famous sonnet, "The New Colossus," welcoming immigrants to the New World.

the Government. The despondency of the secessionists is very marked. They complain of the cream of their country being given up without a struggle, & the little preparation made for its defense. They say their only hope now is with Magruder who they look for from Texas with a body of thirteen thousand men. He Cant (have?) raised half the number. That they may receive reinforcements from Texas is true, but they have a long ways to march over bad roads & poor means of transportation, & before they reach the Red River country it is to be hoped our troops will have permanent possession.

My reception here by the citizens, particularly the creole, has been very kind, & I trust my influence among them will be of benefit to the Government.

I have communicated with Gen Banks & wait his pleasure.

Trusting you're in the enjoyment of good health

Most Respectfully
Your obt Servt

I Zacharie M.D.

AN

ADDRESS

ON THE

DEATH OF ABRAHAM LINCOLN,

PRESIDENT OF THE UNITED STATES,

DELIVERED

BEFORE THE CONGREGATION MIKVE ISRAEL

OF PHILADELPHIA,

AT THEIR SYNAGOGUE IN SEVENTH STREET,

BY THE REV. S. MORAIS,

MINISTER OF THE CONGREGATION,

On Wednesday, April 19, 1865..

PHILADELPHIA:

COLLINS, PRINTER, 705 JAYNE STREET.

1865—5625.

TITLE PAGE OF RABBI SABATO MORAIS ADDRESS

Chapter IV _____

Jews and Slavery in the Old South

Yes, I was a slave, and I'll say this to the whole world; slavery was the worst curse ever visited on the people of the United States.

John Rudds, a slave

Did American Jews perform a uniform position on slavery? To what extent was slavery tolerated? This chapter will deal with some of the experiences of Jews with slavery in the South from 1770-1865.

The colonial period around 1789 was the hey-day of slave importation from Africa and Northern Jews were far more active in this aspect of the slave trade than Southern Jews. During this period, in the small Jewish community of the time, almost every Jewish household of any form, North or South, possessed at least one slave.

No ideological opposition to slavery on the part of Jews during the colonial period existed. This changed when a number of Jews were active in the abolition movement of the 1850s.

I wish to emphasize before I detail some of the activities regarding Jews and slavery that Jews in the nineteenth century were on the periphery of slavery. They did not deal in cotton and tobacco where slavery was predominant. Furthermore the sales of all Jewish slave traders lumped together did not equal that of one gentile farm dominant in the business. I state these points to refute any implications that Jews were a major slave trader.

Only a small number of Jews in the Old South were plantation owners. For one thing, Jews of eastern Europe from whence they came could not own land, and this idea was carried on when they became immigrants. Most immigrants were poor and so the average Southern Jews were either peddlers or storekeepers.

August Bondi

One of the great abolitionists of that era was August Bondi (1833-1907) who came to the United States in 1848, after participating in the failed 1848 Revolutions in Austria and Germany. Bondi moved to the Kansas Territory where he became a partner, with two other Jews, in a general merchandise store. All these men were bitter opponents of slavery, and joined the small band of anti-slavery fighters, led by the famous John Brown. The three, Bondi, Jacob Benjamin, and Theodore Weiner, fought with Brown at the Battle of Black Jack and the Battle of Osawatomic against the pro-slavery forces. I believe John Brown was captured and hung by the state of Virginia with the approval of the national government. It was the Supreme Court of the United States that declared in 1857 that the slave Dred Scott could not sue for his freedom because he was not a person but property. August Bondi was a devout Jew and enlisted in the Union army in 1861 and according to his autobiography he enlisted because *"as a Jehudi I had a duty to perform, to defend the institutions which gave equal rights to all beliefs."*

In the slave trade bartering was a common practice—molasses was traded for rum. Rum was shipped to Africa and bartered for slaves. And then they were bartered back to molasses. The distribution point for slave transactions was out of the West Indies.

The term *"negro"* is used in the context of the times.

It was a mark of respectability owning a slave in the Old South. Anti-Semitism was less in the presence of slaves as the negroes absorbed much of the prejudice that might have been directed against the Jews, had the negroes not been around. More Jews were elected to high office in the South than in the North because of the prevalence of slavery. Jews were able to advance socially and economically by the presence of race distinction which gave superiority to all whites. The existence of slavery gave even to the Jewish peddler a status of equality that otherwise would not have existed.

Slave dealings did not disqualify Jews from receiving the friendship and esteem of their co-religionists any more than it disqualified Christians engaging in business transactions in negro slavery, which was not regarded as incompatible with being a good Jew. Even rabbis dealt with slaves. Jews were among the many Southern citizens who appealed for the apprehension and return of runaway slaves. Crimes of violence against slaves by Jews were probably rare since most of these occurred in rural areas where there were few Jews. But Jews in towns and cities abided by the excessively cruel punishment meted out to blacks who were caught fleeing. Here is an advertisement by one Jew in *"The Louisiana Gazette"* of January 18, 1812:

"20 DOLLARS REWARD

Absconded from the house of the subscribers, on the night of the 16th, a mulatto boy, named Ovid, the property of Judge A. Trouard, about 17 years of age, about five feet high, had a grey colored coatee, with black velvet collar. Whoever will deliver him, or secure him in any jail, shall receive a reward of twenty dollars, besides all reasonable charges. Masters of vessels are forewarned from harboring or carrying said boy at their peril."

None of the major slave traders were Jewish nor did Jews constitute a large portion of traders in the middle of the nineteenth century in any particular community. Jews in the South participated in the buying, owning and selling of slaves along with their neighbors. An advertisement by a Jewish trader, J.F. Moses in 1859 ran as follows:

"NEGRO, NEGROES

The undersigned has just arrived in Lamkin, Virginia, with a likely lot of negroes, about 40 in number, embracing every shade and variety. He has seamstresses, chamber maids, field hands. He has sold over 200 negroes in this section, mostly in this county, and flatters himself that he has so far given satisfaction to his purchases. Being a regular trader in this market he has nothing to gain by misrepresentation, and will, therefore, warrant every negro sold to come up to the bill, squarely and completely. Give him a call at his mart.

J.F. Moses
Lumpkin, Ga, Nov. 14th, 1859"

Jewish masters did not educate their slaves in the Jewish faith and synagogues did not welcome negro worshippers. The Charleston and New Orleans congregations deliberately excluded blacks from membership. The reasons being, blacks had no social standing; they were identified as bondsmen. Fearful of their own acceptance, Jews would do nothing to endanger their standing in racist America; with rare exceptions, Southern Jews were careful to conform to the prevailing attitudes toward slaves and slavery. This seems to contradict some present-day African-Americans who regard themselves as Jews who were descended from slave converts of Jewish masters. On occasion black servants observed Jewish rites and were even buried in Jewish cemeteries. The Richmond congregation required its members to be free, not slaves. There is a contradiction; however, there is a reference to a Jewish negro who was converted to Judaism by his master and was accustomed to attending services at the Charleston synagogue.

Billy Simons (1780-1859) was the only instance of a black Jew in all of the Old South that was recorded.

Slaves in the South had more faith in the Jews than other immigrants as they felt that they had been discriminated and they knew from the Bible that Jews were once slaves and had freed themselves. Even they were told that Benjamin Disraeli was a Jew, a Prime Minister of England. All this to give them encouragement that their day will come. This reminds me of a story about Benjamin Disraeli in reply to a racial slur by Daniel O'Connell in Parliament. *"Yes—I am a Jew and when my ancestors were receiving their Ten Commandments from Mt. Sinai, the ancestors of my opponent were brutal savages herding swine in the forests of Great Britain."* This statement was also attributed to Judah Benjamin, a confederate statesman. However, there was no slavery, even that

Estate Sale—Valuable Negros
BY JACOB OTTOLENGUI.

Will be sold on TUESDAY, the 6th day of January, at "Ryan's Mart," Chalmers street, at 11 o'clock, the following NEGROS, belonging to an estate :

NOVEMBER. aged about 65, a carpenter
JANE, aged 30, a market woman
JANE, aged 25, a cook and house servant
JOSEPH, aged 30, a drayman
BILLY, aged 26, a drayman
SANDY, aged 26, a drayman

The above negros can be seen at my office, 22 Broad street, and treated for at private sale, previous to the day of sale.

Conditions cash ; purchasers to pay for bill of sale.
December 24   Dec. 24 25 29 31 Jan. 1 3 5 6.

Charleston *Courier*, Jan. 1, 1857
(Courtesy of University of Texas Library)

LEWIS B. LEVY,

No. 4 WALL STREET, RICHMOND, VA.

Under the City Hotel,

MANUFACTURER OF ALL KINDS OF

SERVANTS' CLOTHING.

Persons bringing their servants to the city for hire or sale, can be supplied on reasonable terms.

The attention of traders and others particularly solicited.

References : R. H. DICKINSON & BRO.,
      N. B. & C. B. HILL,
      PULLIAM & SLADE,
      BENJAMIN DAVIS.

Richmond Directory for 1852
(Courtesy of Virginia State Library)

BY S. I. & I. I. JONES.

THIS DAY, Feb 6, at 9 o'clock,
At our auction room— 100 sacks white Corn
40 kegs Lard; 10 hlf pipes Cognac Brandy
15 bbls Domestic Brandy; 45 do Gin
30 do Rum; 25 kegs Goshen Butter
50 boxes Absynth and French Cordials
70 boxes Soap; 80 bbls superfine Flour
5 casks Bacon Hams; 50 baskets Champaigne
25 boxes Starch; 10 tierces new Rice
20 bbls dried Beef; 50 kegs Buckwheat
20 m Havana Segars; 10 bbls winter Lamp Oil
40 bbls Monongahela Whisky
25 bbls old Peach Brandy; 50 bxs Sperm Candles
50 boxes Tobacco; 40 bbls Onions——together
with a variety of other goods.
Also—25 cases Boots, Brogans and Shoes.
Also—Dry Goods; Clothing and Fancy articles.
Also.—Negroes at Auction.— Man Alfred, 25 years
old, field hand; Boy Isaac, 7 years old; Woman Ju-
dy, 30 years old and two work Horses. Terms cash.

Administratrix's Sale.
MONDAY, Feb. 8, at 12 o'clock,
At the late Mr. Hopper's Cabinet Ware-room
Royal-street, near Dauphin-street, will be sold th
stock in trade and personal property of said dec' ,
comprising a variety of household Furniture, together with every requisite for a furnishing Un-
dertaker. Terms of sale, 6 months credit, bonds
with approved security.

Mobile *Daily Advertiser and Chronicle,* Feb. 6, 1841
(Courtesy of Duke University Library)

Negroes at Auction.
BY J. & L. T. LEVIN.
WILL be sold, on MONDAY, the 3d January next, at
the Court House, at 10 o'clock,
22 LIKELY NEGROES, the larger number of
which are young and desirable. Among them are Field
Hands, Hostlers and Carriage Drivers, House Servants,
&c., and of the following ages: Robinson 40, Elsey 34,
Yanaky 13, Svlla 11, Anikee 8, Robinson 6, Candy 3.
Infant 9, Thomas 35, Die 38, Amey 18, Eldridge 13,
Charles 6, Sarah 60, Baket 50, Mary 18, Betty 16, Guy
12, Tilla 9, Lydia 24, Rachel 4, Scippio 2.
The above Negroes are sold for the purpose of making
some other investment of the proceeds, the sale will
therefore be positive.
Terms— a credit of one, two and three years, for notes
payable at either of the Banks, with two or more approved
endorsers, with interest from date. Purchasers to pay
for papers.   Dec 8 43
☞ Black River Watchman will copy the above and
forward bill to the auctioneers for payment.

Columbia *Daily South Carolinian,* Dec. 17, 1852
(Courtesy of the South Carolina Library)

COMMITTED to the jail of Powhatan county, on the 2d day of April, a Negro Woman who calls herself JENNY. She fays fhe was raifed by Wm. Gathright, of the county of Henrico, who fold her to Mr. Fulcher, the butcher, of Richmond, and by him fold to one Williamfon, who fold her to one Webfter, of Buckingham, who fold her to a Mr. John Cambell, of King & Queen county, who left her at Lewis Fortine's, a free Negro of this county; from which laft place fhe eloped. She appears to be about the age of 16 or 17, is very black, and has loft fome of her upper fore teeth. The owner is defired to come and prove his property, pay the prifon charges, and take her away, or fhe will be dealt with as the law directs.
           MOSES N. CARDOZO, *Jailor*.
Powhatan Courthoufe, May 17.   3t.

Courtesy of The Jewish Archives of America. Cincinnati, Ohio

Richmond *Enquirer,* May 21, 1805

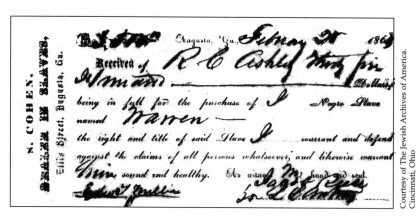

Courtesy of The Jewish Archives of America. Cincinnati, Ohio

Slave Bill of Sale, S. Cohen, 1864

AUCTIONEERS' PRIVATE SALES.

Prime Field Negroes and House Servants.
BY E. MORDECAI, 5 State-street.

At private sale—

TOM, 25 years of age, superior coachman and house servant.

JOHN, 21 years of age, superior coachman and house servant.

LILBURN, 24 years of age, superior coachman and house servant.

ISAAC, 29 years of age, house servant,

DRUCILLA, 20, seamstress, washer and ironer, and house servant.

ELVY, 18, seamstress, washer and ironer, and house servant

AMELIA, 22, seamstress, tailoress, washer, and house servant.

LYDIA, 40, cook, washer and ironer.

LOUISA, 40, cook, washer and ironer.

PATSY, 19, seamstress, cook, washer and ironer, and child's nurse.

CAROLINE, 17 years old, prime field hand.

LUCY, 19 years old, prime field hand.

BETSY, 17 years old, prime field hand.

MARGARET, 16 years old, prime field hand.

CATHERINE, 16 years old, prime field hand.

MILLY, 17 years old, prime field hand.

OCTAVIA, 16 years old, prime field hand.

SALINA, 16 years old, prime field hand.

MARY, 28 years old, prime field hand.

NANCY and 2 children, 20 years old, prime field hand.

SARAH and child, 30 years old, prime field hand.

SUSAN, 30 years old, prime field hand.

SARAH, 18 years old, prime field hand.

CAROLINE, 18 years old, prime field hand.

SAUNDERS, 22, field hand.

BENJAMIN, 25, field hand.

SAMPSON, 30, field hand.

SAM, 16, field hand and plough boy.

MOSES, 33, field hand and cooper.

LINDSAY, 27, field hand.

HENRY, 30, field hand.

ISAAC, 18, field hand.

LAWRENCE, 45, field hand.

BYRON, 22, field hand.

DAVE, 25 years of age, laborer.

NAT, 30 years of age, laborer and sailor.

HENRY, a superior coat, pantaloon and vest maker, 22 years old.

January 1   thmtuwthfm7

Charleston *Courier,* Jan. 1, 1857
(Courtesy of University of Texas Library)

of the Israelites in Egypt, worse than the slavery of the black man in America.

A popular black ballad sung throughout some of the slave communities went as follows:

> *Cruel Jews, jes look at Jesus...*
>
> *Dey nail him to de cross...*
>
> *Dey rivet his feet...*
>
> *Dey hang him high*
>
> *An' dey stretch him wide...*
>
> *O de cruel Jews dun took my Jesus*

In the North most Jews opposed slavery except in New York City where merchants had large dealings with Southern slave owners. New York City was in fact an annex of the South. Jews in New York City who were anti-slavery were threatened with death.

The South was the best customer of New York City. It was said *"our merchants have for sale on their shelves, their principles with their merchandise."* There were many Northern Jewish men with Southern principles.

On the whole, however, Jews were strong unionists and many of them were eager to see the Union preserved. The Jewish Northerners were wary of the anti-slavery extremists, many of whom were evangelical Christians dedicated to the conversion of Jews and the Christianization of the American Constitution. The climate, soil, and types of agriculture made slavery on a large scale unprofitable in the North.

There was an intense pro-slavery feeling in New York City as expressed above. For example, a great orator, Wendell Phillips, delivered an anti-slavery speech on Broadway. The hall was filled with pro-slavery shouters who threw eggs at Mr. Phillips. Tammany Hall held the power of the Democratic party then, which was pro-slavery. There was intense anti-abolition of slavery, a surprise when one considers New York City had more Jews than any other city at that time. In fact if you had anti-slavery feeling it was difficult for any politician to get into public office.

In July 1863, great riots started by the pro-slavery forces—they roamed the street destroying property, burning a negro orphan asylum and killing about thirty negroes. These actions were known as the Draft Riots. This took place after the defeat of the confederates at Gettysburg.

There was one bright Jewish man educated at the college that became Columbia University later and who later had many interviews with Lincoln and aided in his 1864 election, could not obtain a public career because of the anti-slavery feelings. He was ostracized in New York by his acquaintances, and when he became a lawyer, by members of his own family—such was the bitterness of the anti-slavery forces in that part of the country.

A German Jew arrived in 1845, at a time of the great German migration to this country. He recorded his shock at the first sight of a negro being whipped upon his bare back by an overseer and at times with salt and turpentine on the wounds. He noted that the sight of a human being punished in this manner was very repugnant. He got accustomed to this afterward, nevertheless.

Pro-slavers and abolitionists used the readings of the Scriptures to support their ideas. They divided along class, social and political lines as did the rest of the population, most of whom venerated the Bible. The North usually appealed to the teaching of the New Testament and the South denied the existence of any authority other than the Bible.

A New York rabbi, Morris Raphall, before Congregation B'nai Jeshurun in January 1861 claimed that the Bible in his defense of slavery mentioned slavery such as *"thy shall not covet thy neighbor's house or his male slave etc."* He claimed, *"How dare you (the abolitionists) denounce slave holding as a sin in the face and protection afforded slave projects in the 10 Commandments. If you reply 'oh in their time slave holding was lawful now it has become a sin' I reply when and by what authority you draw the line. Tell us precisely the time when slave holdings ceased to be permitted and became sinful."*

He continued, *"If our Northern fellow citizens would recognize these facts there would be less ill feelings toward their Southern brethren."*

Rabbi David Einhorn (1809-1879), a prominent Baltimore Reform rabbi, opposed slavery, for which he was forced to flee to Philadelphia. He was born in Bavaria where he received an Orthodox training and an excellent Hebrew education before drifting into the liberal religious camp. He had already made enemies in his congregation who were pro-slavery. After all, Maryland was a slave state. He felt the Know Nothing party of his day and slavery were the same thing, evil. This Baltimore rabbi found Raphall's speech on slavery reactionary and against Judaism. He was very eager to rebuke Rabbi Raphall. At first he hesitated to come out publicly; it was improper for Rabbis to talk politics in the pulpit, and slavery was a very delicate issue. He could not keep quiet. He just had to attack Raphall. He answered Rabbi Raphall as follows:

"But to proclaim slavery in the name of Judaism to be a God sanctioned institution—the Jewish religious press must raise objections to this, if it does not want itself and Judaism branded forever. Had a Christian clergyman in Europe delivered the Raphall address—the Jewish Orthodox as well as Jewish Reform press would have called the wrath of heaven and earth upon such falsehoods—are we in America to ignore this mischief done by a Jewish preacher? Only such Jews who prize the dollar more highly than their God and their religion can demand or even approve of this."

A Jewish newspaper in the North editorially declared that the rights of the Jewish people as a whole would be undermined by a victory of the slave holders. They appealed for the support of the Union, declaring, *"Stand by the flag."* A Southern Jewish newspaper in reply to this editorial denounced the editorial as a *"black Republican paper."* Republicans of that day were the party of Lincoln and the abolitionists.

Later on, the officers of the Baltimore synagogue asked him

to return with the understanding that he be silent. Because this was a promise he could not keep, and because he did not want to make trouble for his friends, he remained in Philadelphia and became a spiritual leader in Congregation Keneseth Israel.

Even a prominent Jew went to England to appeal to Baron de Rothschild, a member of Parliament, not to support the Southern cause as many Southerners were sent to England begging for support. The English were opposed to slavery and did not give support to the South.

Interracial cohabitation, or miscegenation, was quite common. It was quite difficult to determine the extent by Jews in miscegenation because of the difficulty of distinguishing Jewish names from non-Jewish names. There were so many Jewish names borne by negroes. Many negroes took their names from their Jewish masters or neighbors or many cases from the Bible. Many like Aaron, Abraham, Benjamin, and David could have been either Jewish or gentile. Documentary evidence of this cohabitation was not too many. In one unusual case a body of a grandson of a Jew was exhumed to determine his race in order to determine the extent of miscegenation. This possibly had to do with benefactors of a will. I can recite one case of a Jew who was indicted for *"outraging the decency of society...by cohabiting together...as man and wife, without being lawfully married."*

Some Jews were desperately eager to provide for their slaves because of very special relations. The women were mistresses; the children were their own. Isaac Judah of Richmond raised two free mulatto boys; Isaac Rodriguez, a Pennsylvanian, emancipated a mulatto girl and left her a legacy. Some of these "Jewish children" became very active politicians, men like the Cardozos; members of the same family as the later Associate Justice of the United States Supreme Court, Benjamin Nathan Cardozo.

Here are some comments from Jews on slavery in the South.

Solomon Cohen, who lost a son in the war, wrote, *"I believe that the institution of slavery was refining and civilizing to the whites, giving them an elevated sentiment and ease and dignity of manners only attainable in societies under the restraining influence of a privileged class and at the same time the only human institution that could elevate the negro from barbarism and develop the small amount of intellect with which he is endowed. The reason the Almighty made a colored black is to prove their inferiority."* Today there is still some of this sentiment.

There is a story of a young Jewish boy from the Lower East Side who joined the Confederate army. He came to believe in slavery, took part in many battles, including Gettysburg. This young Jewish Southerner wrote in his diary at the end of the war that *"our cause is lost, comrades who had given their lives for the independence of the South have died in vain."* He continued, *"I do not regret what I have done to cripple the North."*

A Jewess, Eleanor H. Cohen, recorded in her diary:

"Slavery is done away, our noble Jeff Davis as well as all of our great men, are prisoners, Confederate money is worthless. How it makes my blood boil to see them in our streets. Yes—we are again in the hated Union and over us floats the banner that is now the sign of tyranny and oppression." (Shades of *"Gone With The Wind"*)

"I, who believe in the institution of slavery, regret deeply its being abolished. I am accustomed to have them wait on me and I dislike white servants very much."

She continued *"Politically I have much to say. No peace yet agreed upon, but negotiations are being carried on, and people generally think peace will follow. Abraham Lincoln was assassinated in the Washington theatre by a man (John Wilkes Booth) who exclaimed "Death to traitors; Virginia is avenged." So our worst enemy is laid low and (Secretary of State William H. Seward) the arch fiend, was also stabbed and today we hear glorious tidings that the Yankee Congress had a row and (Vice President) Andy Johnson was killed. God grant so may all our foes perish!"* Of course, the latter part of this diary is false.

Today, her romantic writing seems unreal and ridiculous; in her generation her euphoric enthusiasm was typical of the cultured, aristocratic women of her state. Her diary is of particular

Courtesy of The Jewish Archives of America,
Cincinnati, Ohio

Eleanor H. Cohen

Courtesy of The Jewish Archives of America,
Cincinnati, Ohio

Eugenia Phillips
(Mrs. Philip Phillips)

significance because of the many insights it offers into the psyche of a confederate patriot, (although Jewish) in the last days of the war. Eleanor Cohen had four children and died at an early age of thirty-five.

In sharp contrast, there existed the only active and prominent Jewess abolitionist in the United States, Ernestine Rose. She was born in Piotrkow, Poland in 1810, the daughter of a rabbi. Rebelling against the orthodoxy of the Polish Jewry and against Judaism itself, she left home at the age of sixteen and by the time she was twenty-five had become a reformer, an advocate of free thinking, free schools, universal peace and legal equality with men. As an emancipator she was concerned to bring freedom to all people, to women, and certainly to negroes. *"Slavery is not to belong to yourself,"* she said.

Judah P. Benjamin (1811-1884), pictured on this Confederate two-dollar bill, was a prominent Southern lawyer and close friend of Confederate President Jefferson Davis. Benjamin served in the Confederate government as attorney general, secretary of war, and secretary of state.

Some Southern Jews did not deceive themselves into thinking that negro slaves were perfectly happy. A Major Alfred Mordecai of the US army purchased a slave simply to emancipate him though he did nothing to oppose slavery. He resigned his commission rather than fight for the North and did not fight for the South.

General Lee gave an order before the Jewish New Year granting a furlough to each Israelite to go to Richmond for the holidays, a sign that, perhaps, anti-Semitism was not very prevalent in the South.

Judas P. Benjamin, one of the leading Jews in the Confederacy, was the Secretary of State and Treasurer under the Confederacy. He had urged immediate secession in 1861. He was a Louisiana legislator, plantation and slave owner and a US Senator. His interest in Jewish life was negligible. He and David Levy, the Florida politician, intermarried with Christians and abandoned Jewish life. Untold immigrants in every generation made the same

Courtesy of The Jewish Archives of America, Cincinnati, Ohio

Judah P. Benjamin's Plantation House at Bellechasse
Photographed in 1947 by Stuart Lynn, New Orleans

choice. Senator Benjamin rarely, if ever, took up a case where Jews may have been discriminated and appeals made.

Anti-Semites both in the Confederacy and the Union North used the fact that he was a Jew as a club to beat the Jews. He was appointed to be a Justice of the US Supreme Court but wanted to stay in the Senate. As long as he was born a Jew he was the butt of many anti-Semitic diatribes even though he practically was not a Jew because he never admitted it, I believe. Benjamin had to pay the price of his birth. Rabbi Korn thought he had significance for the Jewish community. He stated he was a symbol of American democratic practice as it functioned in the life of a member of the Jewish religious community. He continued that Judah Benjamin achieved greater political power than any other Jew in American History. Well, maybe.

Because the Confederacy was losing the war, some of the leaders like Mr. Benjamin suggested the slaves, more an obstacle to their cause, should be enlisted and then freed. He wrote to a Southern newspaper, *"It is well known that General Lee, who commands so largely the confidence of the people, is strongly in favor of our using the negroes for defense and emancipating them, if necessary, for that purpose."* This may have led President Lincoln to promulgate the Emancipation Proclamation.

At the war's end he was the only major leader of the Confederacy who went into exile to England where he practiced law and died. Attached is a copy of a Confederate two-dollar bill with Mr. Benjamin's picture.

Some excerpts of a will of Isaiah Isaacs of Virginia, August 30, 1803:

> *"Being of opinion that all men are by nature are equally free and being possessed of some of those who are unfortunate doomed to slavery, as to them I must enjoin upon my executors a strict observance of the following clause in my will. My slaves, hereafter named, are to be and they are hereby manumitted and made free so that after the different periods hereafter mentioned, they shall enjoy*

all the privileges and immunities of freed people. My slave, Rachel, is to go free and quit all manner of servitude from and after the first of January, which shall be in the year of one thousand and eight hundred and sixteen. James, from and after the first of January which shall be in the year of 1820. Each of my slaves are to receive the value of twenty dollars in clothing the day of their manumission."

Since manumissions were frowned upon in some southern states, testators circumvented the law by providing special treatment for slaves. They made liberal bequests to their heirs who were enjoined never to sell them and were urged to treat them with leniency.

The history of slavery would not have mattered much from historic reality if no single Jew had been resident in the South. Other whites would have owned slaves; other traders and auctioneers would have bought and sold slaves.

The idea proposed by anti-Semites, that Jews were the major slave traders, does not bear up to the facts. The Jews in the south were, for the most part, peddlers, and poor immigrants and being mostly urban people, owned but few of the many plantations where slavery existed. And I repeat what I stated previously; the sales of all Jewish Slave Traders lumped together did not equal that of one gentile plantation dominant in the business.

THE STOCKING THIEF.

Epilogue

American history is relatively unknown amongst Jews, let alone others. They participated in many actions during the Revolution and throughout the Civil War. President Lincoln was a great friend of the Jewish people. His rapid revocation of the anti-Semitic Order No. 11 of General Grant and his influence in obtaining Jewish chaplains in the army are items Jews can be proud of this President. His statement *"I do not like to hear a class or nationality condemned on account of a few sinners"* is the basis for refuting all forms of racism. He knew of no distinction between Jew and gentile.

President Lincoln's actions in behalf of the Jews caused Congress to recognize the principle of equality. Equally so, American Jewry knew that it need have no hesitation about using the rights of petition. Its faith in the American safeguards of religious minorities was upheld.

President Washington's letter to the Rhode Island synagogue, *"The government of the United States which gives to bigotry no sanction, to persecution no assistance"* is something all American Jewry can also be proud of. This letter of Washington and other similar letters he wrote to the synagogues at that time have been used to confront those who espouse anti-Semitism and other bigotry.

This exchange of letters between the congregations and President Washington was a realization of their new dignity and status. Their status improved over the years and today they are no longer tradesmen and merchants but lawyers and professionals exerting considerable influence politically and economically.

The question of the morality of slavery was rarely questioned in the mid-eighteenth and nineteenth centuries. It was determined by the business relations at the time. There were always some who questioned the morality of slavery.

President George Washington had slaves, as did James Madison as well as most of our Founding Fathers. Those were the times. One need not conclude any ethical position for slavery during the early years of America.

How true is all this history about the negro may be deemed from the following, a former slave:

"In all the books that you have studied, you never have studied negro history, have you? You studied about the Indians and white folks, but what did they tell you about the negro? If you want negro history, you will have to get it from some body who wore the shoe, and by and by, from one to the other, you will get a book."

(J. Reed, former slave)

The above statement can be applied to Jewish history in the period 1770-1865. One can search all the history textbooks on the Civil War and never would you find a mention of Dr. I. Zacharie, whom Lincoln had trusted with great confidence, except by Dr. Bertram Korn from whom I have quoted extensively.

Today, Jewish behavior on race is full of dilemmas and contradictions. Judaism, as a religious tradition, flatly rejects racism; but Jews as individuals are prone to racial bigotry as reflected in the use of the Yiddish epithet *"schvartz."* Jews rarely resort to violence or overt meanness when blacks or Hispanics move into the neighborhood, but Jews have fled the cities in a massive post-World War II exodus, moving to suburbs which are usually all white.

If not for the extensive research, fortitude and work of Bertram Korn in his book, *"American Jewry and the Civil War,"* Morris U. Schappes in his book *"The Documentary History of the Jews in the United States"* and the works of Jacob Marcus, I doubt if we would have ever known of President Lincoln's beneficence to the Jew.

Today, blacks and Jews, despite everything, seem to share a common vision of a just, generous, open society. We vote more alike than any other racial or religious groups. We both recoil from any smell of bigotry.

From official statistics as reported in the Jewish Directory and Almanac 1986, the Jews furnished soldiers and high officers to the Revolution, the War of 1812 and the Mexican War. In the Civil War he was represented in the armies and navies of both the North and the South by 10% of his numerical strength.

The Newport synagogue, dedicated in 1763. The school building on the left, added at the insistence of the Jewish community, compromised the Palladian exterior.

Photograph courtesy of the American Jewish Historical Society.

Photograph courtesy of the American Jewish Historical Society.

The interior of the Newport synagogue.

*"The Hebrew Purim Ball at the Academy of Music, March 14."
Frank Leslie's Illustrated Newspaper (1 April 1865). Courtesy of the
Library of Congress.*

*Nineteenth-century American Jews widely celebrated Purim, both by the
giving of charity and the merriment of parties and costumes. Costumes worn
here were both specifically Jewish, like the dreidel (the top with Hebrew
letters), and typical of American balls. The artist indulges in stereotypical
images, giving several partygoers exaggerated hooked noses.*

Kehilat Kodesh B'nai Yeshurun (Plum Street Synagogue), Cincinnati. Dedicated in 1865, this Moorish-style synagogue embodied its rabbi Isaac Mayer Wise's aspirations for American Jews and Judaism.

Bibliography

1. *Documentary History of Jews in the United States* by Morris U. Schappes. Pages 63-66, 80-81, 99-102, 150-157, 375-388, 395-397, 405-418, 444-448, 436, 437, 472, 473, Stocken Press, 1971.

2. *American Jewry in the Civil War* by Bertram Korn, Jewish Publication Society.

3. *Unrecognized Patriots of the Jew in the American Revolution* by Samuel Reznick, Greenwood Press 1975. Pages 41, 82-83, 143, 144-146, 149.

4. *Early American Jews* by Jacob Marcus. Publication of the American Jewish Archives.

5. *A Time for Planting* by Eli Faber Publication of the American Historical Society.

6. *Eventful Years and Experience* by Bertram Korn, The Jewish Archives.

7. *Collection of Robert Todd Lincoln* Letters from the Library of Congress, Manuscript Division.

8. *Abraham Lincoln — The Tribute of the Synagogue*, by Hertz, Block Publishing Co. 1927.

9. *The American Jew* by Simon Wolf.

10. *Essays in American Jewish History* by Jacob Marcus. American Jewish Archives.

Appendix A

*Zacharie-Lincoln Correspondence**

St. Charles Hotel
New Orleans Jany 14th 1863

To his Excellency
A Lincoln President
of the United States

Dear Sir

In my last communication I promised to give you further details related to Genl Butler & now embrace the opportunity.

What I now relate I get from one of the party in person. Several Gentlemen were called before Genl Butler to further some certain purpose of his, to which they would not however agree, when as a threat he told that by a wave of his hand from the top of the St Charles Hotel he could make New Orleans a second St Domingo, and it it suited his purpose he would yet make the Streets of the City run with blood.

I now relate a pecuniary transaction. Messer Hyde & Goodrich the principal Jewelers here, remited to a relation in the City check on one of the Banks for five thousand dollars, payable to a relation here by the name of Norton, the proceeds of the check to be paid over to the clerks in their establishment for salary due. The letter containing the afore mentioned check fell into the hands of Genl Butler, who sent for Mr Norton, who he made endorse the check under threat of sending him to Fort Jackson. The check was paid, but is there any record of how the money was applied? I know another transaction for twenty one hundred dollars of the same kind.

Mr. I P Davis President of the Bank of New Orleans, one of the most esteemed gentlemen of this city, who Genl Butler threatened with hanging, & who he confined in a criminals cell for over two weeks, has entirely lost his mind. This is looked upon here by all classes of people as an unjustifiable act of severity.

Some parties robbed the Jesuit church of two sets silver candellabras & other silver articles. The day after Genl Banks took command they were returned.

May the great Author of worlds grant you all happiness–an uninterrupted series of health–addition of years to the number of your days and a continuance of guardianship to that freedom, which, under the auspices of Heaven, your magnanimity and wisdom have given these State.

Yours truly,

I. Zacharie

*All of these letters are taken from manuscript originals in the Robert Todd Lincoln Collection of Lincoln Papers, Manuscript Division, Library of Congress, with two exceptions noted.

Appendix B

To the Hebrew-Congregation of the City of Savannah

Gentlemen,

I thank you with great sincerity for your congratulations on my appointment to the office, which I have the honor to hold by the unanimous choice of my fellow-citizens: and especially for the expressions which you are pleased to use in testifying the confidence that is reposed in me by your congregation.

As the delay which has naturally intervened between my election and your address has afforded an opportunity for appreciating the merits of the federal-government, and for communicating your sentiments of its administration—I have rather to express my satisfaction than regret at a circumstance, which demonstrates (upon experiment) your attachment to the former as well as approbation of the latter.

I rejoice that a spirit of liberality and philanthropy is much more prevalent than it formerly was among the enlightened nations of the earth; and that your brethren will benefit thereby in proportion as it shall become still more extensive. Happily the people of the United States of America have, in many instances, exhibited examples worthy of imitation—the salutary influence of which will doubtless extend much farther, if gratefully enjoying those blessings of peace which (under favor of Heaven) have been obtained by fortitude in war, they shall conduct themselves with reverence to the Deity, and charity towards their fellow-creatures.

May the same wonder-working Deity, who long since delivering the Hebrews from their Egyptian Oppressors planted them in the promised land—whose providential agency has lately been conspicuous in establishing these United States as an independent nation—still continue to water them with the dews of Heaven and to make the inhabitants of every denomination participate in the temporal and spiritual blessings of that people whose God is Jehovah.

G. Washington

To the Hebrew Congregations in the Cities of Philadelphia, New York, Charleston and Richmond

Gentlemen,

The liberal sentiment towards each other which marks every political and religious denomination of men in this country stands unrivalled in the history of nations—The affection of such a people is a treasure beyond the reach of calculation; and the repeated proofs which my fellow citizens have given of their attachment to me, and approbation of my doings form the purest source of my temporal felicity—The affectionate expressions of your address again excite my gratitude, and receive my warmest acknowledgements.

The power and goodness of the Almighty were strongly manifested in the events of our late glorious revolution—and his kind interposition in our behalf has been no less visible in the establishment of our present equal government—In war he directed the sword—and in peace he has ruled in our councils—my agency in both has been guided by the best intentions, and a sense of the duty which I owe my country: and as my exertions hitherto have been amply rewarded by the approbation of my fellow-citizens, I shall endeavor to deserve a continuance of it by my future conduct.

May the same temporal and eternal blessings which you implore for me, rest upon your congregations.

G. Washington

From the Newport Congregation to the President of the United States, August 17, 1790.

Sir,

Permit the Children of the Stock of Abraham to approach you with the most cordial affection and esteem for your person and merits—and to join with our fellow-citizens in welcoming you to New Port.

With pleasure we reflect on those days—those days of difficulty and danger, when the God of Israel, who delivered David from the peril of the sword—shielded your head in the day of battle:—and we rejoice to think that the same Spirit, who rested in the bosom of the greatly beloved Daniel, enabling him to preside over the Provinces of the Babylonish Empire, rests, and ever will rest upon you, enabling you to discharge the arduous duties of Chief Magistrate in these States.

Deprived as we have hitherto been of the invaluable rights of free citizens, we now, (with a deep sense of gratitude to the Almighty Disposer of all events) behold a Government, [(] erected by the Majesty of the People) a Government which to bigotry gives no sanction, to persecution no assistance—but generously affording to All liberty of conscience, and immunities of citizenship—deeming every one, of whatever nation, tongue, or language equal parts of the great governmental machine. This so ample and extensive federal union whose basis is Philanthropy, mutual confidence, and public virtue, we cannot but acknowledge to be the work of the Great God, who ruleth in the armies of Heaven, and among the inhabitants of the Earth, doing whatsoever seemeth him good.

For all the blessings of civil and religious liberty which we enjoy under an equal and benign administration we desire to send up our thanks to the Antient of days, the great Preserver of Men—beseeching him that the Angel who conducted our forefathers through the wilderness into the promised land, may graciously conduct you through all the dangers and difficulties of this mortal life—and when like Joshua full of days, and full of honor, you are gathered to your Fathers, may you be admitted into the heavenly Paradise to partake of the water of life and the tree of immortality.

May the great Author of worlds grant you all happiness—an uninterrupted series of health—addition of years to the number of your days and a continuance of guardianship to that freedom, which, under the auspices of Heaven, your magnanimity and wisdom have given these States.

Levi Sheftal, President
in behalf of the Hebrew-Congregation

Appendix C

My parents were Israelites, and I was nurtured in the faith of my ancestors. In deciding to adhere to it, I have but exercised a right, guaranteed to me by the constitution of my native State, and of the United States—a right given to all men by their Maker—a right more precious to each of us than life itself. But, while claiming and exercising this freedom of conscience, I have never failed to acknowledge and respect the like freedom in others. I might safely defy the citation of a single act, in the whole course of my official career, injurious to the religious rights of any other person. Remembering always that the great mass of my fellow-citizens were Christians; profoundly grateful to the Christian founders of our republic, for their justice and liberality to my long persecuted race; I have earnestly endeavored, in all places and circumstances, to act up to the wise and tolerant spirit of our political institutions. I have therefore been careful to treat every Christian, and especially every Christian under my command, with exemplary justice and ungrudging liberality. Of this, you have had clear proof, so far as my command of the Vandalia is concerned, from the lips of Lieutenants [Edmund] Lanier and [John N.] Maffit. They testify to the observance, on board that ship, under the standing rules and regulations prescribed by me, of the Christian Sabbath, and to the scrupulous regard paid by me on all occasions, to the religious rights and feelings of the officers and men.

I have to complain—more in sorrow than in anger do I say it—that in my official experience I have met with little to encourage, though with much to frustrate, these conciliatory efforts. At an early day, and especially from the time when it became known to the officers of my age and grade, that I aspired to a lieutenancy, and still more, after I had gained it, I was forced to encounter a large share of the prejudice and hostility by which, for so many ages, the Jew has been pursued. I need not speak to you of the incompatibility of these sentiments with the genius of Christianity, or the precepts of its author. You should know this far better than I; but I may ask you to unite with the wisest and best men of our own country and of Europe, in denouncing them, not merely as injurious to the peace and welfare of the community, but as repugnant to every dictate of reason, humanity and justice.

In February, 1818, I was transferred, by Commodore [Charles] Stewart, from his ship, the Franklin, 74, to the frigate United States, under the command of Captain [William M.] Crane. Under the influence of the double prejudice to which I have alluded, a conspiracy was formed among certain officers of this frigate to prevent my reception in her. Commodore [T.A.C.] Jones, in answer to the eighth interrogatory on my part, give a full account of it. He says:

"Lieutenant Levy, for several months, was fourth, and I first lieutenant, of the frigate United States, where he discharged his duty satisfactorily to the captain as well as to the first lieutenant, notwithstanding his advent into our ship was attended with such novel and discouraging circumstances as, in justice to captain Levy, renders it necessary here to record them.

"On the arrival of the Franklin, of 74 guns, at Syracuse, in 1818, bearing the broad pennant of commodore Charles Stewart, to relieve commodore [John S.] Chauncey, then in command of the Mediterranean squadron, it was understood that lieutenant Levy, a supernumerary on board of the Franklin, was to be ordered to the frigate United States, then short of her complement of lieutenants. Whereupon, the *ward-room mess*, without consulting me, determined to remonstrate against Levy's coming aboard. I was called on by a member of the mess to communicate their wishes to Captain Crane and ask his interference.

"Astonished at such a proposition, I inquired as to the cause, when I was answered, that he was a Jew, and not an agreeable person, and they did not want to be brought in contact with him in our then very pleasant and harmonious mess of some eight or nine persons; and, moreover, that he was an interloper, having entered the navy as *master*, to the prejudice of the older midshipmen, &c.,&c.

Such was the reply, in substance, to my inquiry. I then asked the relator if he, or any member of our mess, knew anything, of his own knowledge, derogatory to lieutenant Levy, as an officer and as a gentleman. The answer was *no*, but they had heard thus and so, &c., &c. I endeavored to point out the difficulties that might result from a procedure so much at variance with military subordination, and the justice due to a brother officer, against whom they had nothing but vague and ill-defined rumors; but my counsel then did not prevail. The remonstrance was made directly to captain Crane, and by captain Crane to commodore Stewart. Levy soon after reported on board the frigate United States, for duty. When Lieutenant Levy came on board, he asked a private interview with me, wishing my advice as the proper course he ought to pursue under such embarrassing circumstances. I gave it freely and simply, to the effect, viz.: do your duty as an officer and a gentleman, be civil to all, however reserved you may choose to be to any, and the first man who observes a different course towards you, call him to a strict and prompt account. Our messmates were gentlemen, and having perceived their error before lieutenant Levy got on board, had, in accordance with my previous advice, determined to receive lieutenant Levy as a gentleman and a brother officer, and to respect and treat him as such, till by his conduct he should prove himself unworthy. I continued a few months longer on board the frigate United States, as her first lieutenant, during the whole of which time Lieutenant Levy's conduct and deportment was altogether unexceptionable, and I know that, perhaps with a single exception, those who opposed his joining our mess, not only relented, but deeply regretted the false step they had incautiously taken."

During the few months that Commodore Jones remained in the ship United States, his wise and just counsels had the effect he describes. After he left her, I am sorry to be obliged to say, the old prejudices revived in the breasts of too many of my associates.

In December, 1824, a conspiracy of the same kind was formed among the junior officers of the ward-room mess, on board the North Carolina. She was about to sail for the Mediterranean to join the squadron in that sea; and I was ordered to take passage in

her, and to report myself to Commodore Creighton, the comman-
der-in-chief of the squadron. Commodore Isaac Mayo, one of the
witnesses produced by me, gives a full account of this cabal, and of
his refusal to join it. His testimony will be referred to hereafter, in
another connexion...

In 1844, the President [John Tyler] nominated me to the
Senate for promotion as captain. This nomination was confirmed
on the [31st] day of May, 1844,—my appointment to take rank from
the 29th March, 1844. The circumstances attending this appointment were of peculiar interest to me; and it is most important that
they should be fully understood by the Court. Attempts were
made, outside the Senate, by certain officers of the Navy, to induce
that body to reject my nomination. The naval Committee of the
Senate, to whom the nomination had been referred, were
approached by officers hostile to or prejudiced against me; and
such objections were made to my appointment, that the committee
felt it proper to call on the Secretary of the Navy for all papers on
file relating to my official conduct. The archives of the Department
were ransacked; charges preferred against me during my service as
sailing-master, lieutenant and commander, growing (with a single
exception) out of those petty altercations and personal quarrels
unfortunately too common in our profession, were raked up; and
the records of all the courts martial before which, in the course of
thirty years, I had been brought, were laid before the committee.
These documents having been thoroughly examined by them, they
reported in favor of the nomination; and on their report it was
unanimously confirmed...

When, in 1855, I complained to Secretary [of the Navy,
James C. Dobbin of "some unseen influence" seeking "through
unmerited prejudice to injure me with the Department," and to
prevent it from according to me my just rights, I stated what I then
fully believed, and what I had long before suspected to be the fact.
I was driven to this conclusion by the persistent refusal of the several secretaries to employ me, in the face of all the proofs of my fit-
ness, in the records of the Department, and of the recommenda-
tions and support of so many distinguished men, in support of my

applications. I could draw, from the circumstances, no other inference; nor do I think that any other can be drawn by you. But the fact is not now left to inference merely. You have, in the deposition of the Secretary, Mr. [George] Bancroft, direct evidence of the fact. In answer to the ninth interrogatory on my part, he says:

"When Secretary of the Navy, I never had cause to doubt, and never doubted, Captain Levy's competence to serve the United States in the grade of captain. I did not find myself able to give him a command, for three reasons:

1st. The excessive number of officers of his grade made it impossible to employ all of them who were fit.

2d. The good of the service, moreover, seemed to require bringing forward officers less advanced in years than most of the captains, and the law sanctioned that course.

3d. I perceived a strong prejudice in the service against Captain Levy, which seemed to me, in a considerable part, attributable to his being of the Jewish persuasion; and while I, as an executive officer, had the same liberal views which guided the President and Senate in commissioning him as a captain, I always endeavored in fitting out ships to have some reference to that harmonious co-operation which is essential to the highest effectiveness."

To the first of these reasons no exception can be taken. The second is founded on a favorite theory of Mr. Bancroft, while Secretary, to which, were it impartially carried out, I should be as little disposed to object as any other officer of my rank and age.

The third reason assigned by Mr. Bancroft, though last in order, is not least in importance.

The fact that it is assigned by him as one of the reasons for not giving me a command, justified the inference that the first two reasons would not have been sufficient to produce that result without the addition of the third.

From what source, or in what manner, Mr. Bancroft perceived the strong prejudice in the service against me, of which he speaks, he does not state. But it is easy to trace it to its origin. He had never been officially connected with the Navy until he came to Washington in 1845, as head of the Department. He was then brought into intercourse with such officers of the Navy as were enabled, by their rank, their connection with bureaux, or their social position, to cultivate the acquaintance, and get the ear of the secretary. It was only by means of such intercourse, that it was possible for him to become acquainted with the prejudices which existed in the service against any of its members. It was only in this way that he could learn that any such prejudice existed against me. Among the officers of the Navy to whom the secretary was thus peculiarly accessible, there were some who were friendly to me; but there were others who were not only unfriendly, but also active and bitter in their hostility against me. How else than through intercourse with those who had the motive, and took the pains, to force it upon him, was it possible for Mr. Bancroft to know that any prejudice existed against me in the Navy; and how could he form any estimate as to its strength, except from the frequency and rancour with which it was obtruded upon his notice?

From the same source which informed him of the prejudice, he learned its nature and grounds—the chief, if not the sole ground, being my peculiar religious faith—my "being of the Jewish persuasion." Doubtless, those who could make such a fact the pretext for a prejudice against a brother officer, so inveterate and unyielding, as to compel the head of the department reluctantly to recognise and admit as—to some extent at least—an element of his official action, would not scruple to disparage and traduce, in other respects, the object of their aversion. But even their efforts failed to awaken, for a moment, in the mind of the secretary, a solitary doubt as to my *competence*. This he tells us in the most emphatic terms.

In the satisfaction which this avowal gives me—in the gratitude I owe, and shall ever cherish, to one who, in spite of such efforts, retained towards me an opinion so favorable—I could almost pass over, without remark, the injury done me—most unwittingly, I am sure—by his allowing to such an objection any weight whatever. Had it then come to my knowledge, I could have shown him, just as I have now shown to you, from the records of the department, that during my year's command of the Vandalia, my religious faith never impaired the efficiency of my ship; that I never permitted it to interfere with the rights, or to wound the feelings, of my Christian officers and men; and that I did what I could, and all that they desired, to respect and satisfy those rights and feelings. I might have shown to him, as I have shown to you, by the evidence of the many officers, who, in this investigation, have testified in my behalf, that the prejudice to which he was constrained to give such serious effect against me, was far from being so general or so strong as he was led to believe;—that officers, more in number than my traducers, and far better qualified to judge, were untainted by it—treated it with contempt, and denounced it as inconsistent with the spirit of our institutions—unworthy of the present age, and degrading to the honor of the naval service. And I might thus, perhaps, have afforded him the opportunity, which, I doubt not, he would gladly have seized, not only from a sense of justice to myself, but in accordance with his own liberal and enlightened convictions, of setting his face, like a flint, against the double-headed hydra of personal prejudice and religious bigotry, and of driving it forever from the councils of his department. The benefit of such an act to myself would have been insignificant, in comparison with the vindication it would have furnished of the dignity and justice of our Government, and its faithful conservation of the most sacred of our public and private rights...

Mr. President and Gentlemen of the Court:

My defence, so far as it depends on the examination of the evidence, is before you; and here, perhaps, I ought to stop. But the peculiarities of my case—the importance and far-reaching interest of the principles it involves—requires, what I hope you will allow me, a few additional remarks.

That the allegation of unfitness for the naval service, made against me by the Government, was wholly unsupported by evidence; and that I have made out a complete defence against the attempt to justify my dismissal, and an affirmative title to restoration, by the proofs on my part; these I regard as undeniable propositions. And yet there are those connected with the navy, who, notwithstanding all the proofs I have produced, are hostile to my restoration. This, it would be vain to deny to others, or to conceal from myself. Should any one of these dare to obtrude upon you the opinion or the wish, that I should not be restored; or, being restored, should not be placed upon the active list; you have only to refer him to the oath which you have taken, to silence and rebuke him. Permit me—not that I suppose you can have forgotten its terms, but because of their peculiar pertinency to my case—to quote the closing words of this oath. It not only requires you, as before remarked "well and truly to examine and inquire, according to the evidence, into the matter now before you;" but, to do this, "without partiality or prejudice." This oath, although exceedingly brief, is exceedingly comprehensive and precise. The lawmakers who framed it well knew the special dangers to which Courts of Inquiry are exposed—partiality toward influential prosecutors and accusers, and prejudice against the accused. Against these, the oath solemnly warns you; and if ever there was a case in which such a warning was right and seasonable, this is that case.

The Government, with its vast power and influence, is, in name at least, my prosecutor. Men in high places, who have once done me grievous wrong, are interested to prevent the remedying of that wrong. There are others, not without their influence, who, by their activity in support of the wrong, and in opposition to the remedy, have a common interest with my prosecutors.

Never, on the other hand, was there a man, in the ranks of our profession, against whom, in the breasts of certain members of that profession, prejudices so unjust and yet so strong, have so long and so incessantly rankled. Such, too, are the origin and character of these prejudices, as to make them, of all others, the most inveterate and unyielding. The prejudice felt by men of little minds, who think themselves, by the accidental circumstances of wealth or ancestry, better than the less favored of their fellows; the prejudice of *caste*, which looks down on the man who, by honest toil, is the maker of his own fortunes; this prejudice is stubborn as well as bitter, and of this I have had, as you have seen by the proofs, my full share. But this is placable and transient compared with that generated and nourished by religious intolerance and bigotry.

The first article of the amendments to the Constitution of the United States, specially declares, in its first clause, that "Congress shall make no law respecting an establishment of religion, or prohibiting the free exercise thereof;" thus showing by its place, no less than by its language, how highly freedom of conscience was valued by the founders of our Republic. In the constitutions of the several States, now in force, the like provision is contained. Our liberality and justice, in this regard, have been honored by the friends of liberty and human rights throughout the world. An eminent British writer, about thirty years ago, in the ablest of their reviews, used, in reference to this point, the following language:

"They have fairly and completely, and probably forever, extinguished that spirit of religious persecution which has been the employment and the curse of mankind, for four or five centuries; not only that persecution which imprisons and scourges for religious opinions, but the tyranny of incapacitation, which by disqualifying from civil offices, and cutting a man off from the lawful objects of ambition, endeavors to strangle religious freedom in silence, and to enjoy all the advantages, without the blood, and noise, and fire of persecution. * * * * * * * * * In this particular, the Americans are at the head of all the nations of the world.*"

Little did the author of this generous tribute to our country suspect, that even while he was penning it, there were those in the American navy, with whom it was a question whether a Jew should be tolerated in the service? Still less did he dream, that at the very moment when, in his own country, a representative of the illustrious house of RUSSELL, eminent by his services in the cause of freedom, of education, and of justice, is about giving himself, with the full assent of his government, to the work of Jewish emancipation, a spectacle like the present should be witnessed in this

* Sydney Smith, in Edinburgh Review, July, 1824. [p. 429].

land of equality and freedom. For with those who would now deny to me, because of my religious faith, the restoration, to which, by half a century of witnesses, I have proved myself entitled, what is it but an attempt to place the professors of this faith under the ban of incapacitation?

This is the case before you; and, in this view, its importance cannot be overrated. It is the case of every Israelite in the Union. I need not speak to you of their number. They are unsurpassed by any portion of our people in loyalty to the Constitution and to the Union; in their quiet obedience to the laws; and in the cheerfulness with which they contribute to the public burthens.... How largely do they all contribute to the activities of trade; to the interests of commerce; to the stock of public wealth! Are all these to be proscribed? And is this to be done while we retain in our Constitution the language I have quoted? Is this language to be spoken to the ear, but broken to the hope, of my race? Are the thousands of Judah and the ten thousands of Israel, in their dispersions throughout the earth, who look to America, as a land bright with promise—are they now to learn, to their sorrow and dismay, that we, too, have sunk into the mire of religious intolerance and bigotry? And are American Christians now to begin the persecution of the Jews? Of the Jews, who stand among them the representatives of the patriarchs and prophets;—the Jews, to whom were committed the oracles of God;—the Jews, from whom these oracles have been received, and who are the living witnesses of their truth;—the Jews, from whom came the founder of Christianity;—the Jews, to whom, as Christians themselves believe, have been made promises of greatness and of glory, in whose fulfilment are bound up the hopes, not merely of the remnant of Israel, but of all the races of men?

U. P. LEVY

Appendix D

In the 1930's, when the GEORGE WASHINGTON-ROBERT MORRIS-HAYM SALOMON MEMORIAL was being planned, the *Christian Century* editorially grasped its significance in these words:

> "The Monument...will not have as its primary object, however, honoring of individuals as such but rather the celebrating of the fact that people of many races, appropriately symbolized by this Polish Jew, participated in the war for independence. Americans are accustomed to think of their country as one in which men of many nationalities have found a home; it is important that we be reminded that a number of these nationalities were present from the very beginning and helped lay the foundations of that republic..."

On the day following the dedication of the memorial, the *Chicago Sun* of December 16, 1941, editorially rejoiced that the sculpture stood as a "reminder that Jew and gentile, citizen and statesman, Republican and Democrat, worker and capitalist, built and maintained this Nation."

Six months before the dedication of the memorial, Mayor Edward J. Kelly noted its significance in these words:

> "...it can stand, and will stand, as Chicago's testimonial to the hardiness of the democratic spirit. It will express our recognition that tolerance and brotherly cooperation make for a better city to live in, a better nation to live in, and—someday not too far in the future—a better world to live in."

In the message he sent to Mr. Hodes a month before the dedication, President Roosevelt wrote:

> "The incomparable leadership of Washington would have been nullified without the able support he received from key men in the various stages of the struggle out of which we emerged as a Nation.

> "Two financiers on whom Washington leaned heavily in the darkest hours of the Revolution were Haym Salomon and Robert Morris. Their genius in finance and fiscal affairs and unselfish devotion to the cause of liberty made their support of the utmost importance when the struggling colonies were fighting against such heavy odds.

> "It is, therefore, especially appropriate that this great triumvirate of patriots—George Washington, Robert Morris and Haym Salomon—should be commemorated together in Chicago. The memorial which you are about to dedicate will stand as an inspiration to generations yet unborn to place love of country above every selfish end."